Develo

M000268635

Supernatural abilities

Technical Guide
in Oriental Esoteric Traditions

By Maha Vajra

F.Lepine Publishing

Copyright 2008

ISBN: 978-0-9809415-5-5

www.MahaVajra.BE

Table of Contents

Introduction

Although everyone may start practicing the techniques found in this book, the ESP training will be more efficient for those who have at least 100 non-linear hours of experience with meditation. However, the training will still work if the student practices meditation along the way, even if it is for the first time. For this purpose, we will have a short chapter on meditation. So that everyone is comfortable with this training, we will suggest a few meditative techniques of various spiritual traditions. We encourage the reader to be open-minded to all spiritual paths, while engaging in his preferred tradition.

Any type of technical training can take up to two years, in just about any field of application (cooking, building, machinery operator...). It is the same for ESP. Although most people will show small scale results right from the beginning, it can take up to two years of daily practice to get efficient results. Most people will step quickly thru the techniques, as fast as possible, hoping to develop ESP quicker. This haste will be their downfall, since the body, the mind and the consciousness will not have time to entrain. I encourage everyone to practice long enough each technique before moving on to the other. Along with your training, you are also encouraged to have meditation periods, where you are not entraining yourself to ESP. These meditations are essential breaks you must give to your mind. Failure to meditate will result in longer training requirements before any sign of success shows up.

Some people find the recitation of mantras (like magic formulas) to be inefficient, or meditation to be a waste of time. When asked how long they recited the mantra, they answer with a few minutes, 1 hour to the most. When asked how long they meditated, they reply that they could not endure past the first 20 minutes. It takes serious devotion and discipline to do this training, but once done, it is extremely powerful and works wonders. The mind and the body will react to this training. Sometimes positively, sometimes apparently negatively, while the structures of your consciousness change and adopt new tools to interact with the universe at every level.

Later on, we will learn how to produce an experience of peace in someone else, to regenerate the body, to see at a distance by placing your point of view anywhere you wish, and much more. This is only possible if every step of the training is done properly, with a mala in hand (explained later), with the good number of recitation of each mantra implicated in the training of such supernatural power. If it was so easy to develop supernatural abilities, we would see mages and vampires roaming around the streets at night. Only those with dedication to their training will succeed.

Of course, there are many other ways to develop supernatural abilities or extra-sensory perception, but this method is proven to work with those who have the patience and do each step with determination. The attitude also has a great influence on the training. The more positive you think about your training, the faster the effects will come. Someone who was lucky enough to experience a supernatural phenomena will find it easier during his training, since his mind won't fight all along the way, doubting in the possibilities. While those who did not yet experience their first "weird" sensation, or random telepathic communication, will have to keep a constant focus on obtaining success. The mind has a great deal to play in the success of this training.

Not only must we keep a positive and determined attitude, we must also train our mind into becoming clear like calm water. Thus, we start the training by clearing the mind. For this, we will use a technique called "japa" that consists of chanting or reciting a "mantra" using a bead necklace to count the exact number of repetitions. The bead necklace is called a "mala".

The human system is not only made of flesh and bones. We are also made of emotions, thoughts, and pure thought, that I like to call "Consciousness". This consciousness is not only the fact that I am aware of what is going on. Consciousness also refers to a relationship with all the planes of existence: physical, vital, emotional, mental, causal, soul, spirit.

The human identity, also called the "ego", is made up of:
- Physical / Animal body
- Vital / Energy body
- Astral / Emotional body
- Mental / Mind body

The higher identity, that I call the "Self" is your:
- Causal / Consciousness body
- Soul
- Spirit

The ego and the Self are not separated. But we attribute the four first parts of our identity to the "ego" because the body, energies, emotions and thoughts are affected by the natural laws and the animal instincts. While the Self, which is consciousness, soul and Spirit, is free from the influence of the animal instinct; it is our true origin.

Let us start right away with one of the tools that we will use to entrain our human nature (ego) to collaborate with our spiritual nature (Self).

Charging a Mantra

Before we can get to the next step, it will be important to learn how to clear the mind, and how to charge a mantra. It is essential to develop the habit to clear the mind before attempting any ESP experience. The human ego tends to send images to the diaphane (explained later), using our imagination. We have to learn how to reduce these interferences, but also to see thru them, in order to perceive the subtle nature of spiritual perception.

It is believed that this ESP training can be hard on your mind. In fact, it is your mind that will be hard on your training. We need to go beyond the limits where your mind will cooperate with the techniques. When we don't think for a while, the mind becomes agitated and wants attention. Lots of attention. It then does all it can to disturb your training, and make you lose your focus. The first technique aims at going beyond this mental limit, and training your mind into stillness.

The technique that we suggest to clear the mind is to do mantra recitation, while using a mala; a technique called japa, in Sanskrit. Although we suggest the use of a mala (Hindu or Buddhist prayer necklace), it is not an absolute requirement. Only, the use of a mala will make the training more efficient, and will also transform your mala into a "power item" while you train. You can find a 108 or 109 bead mala in most oriental stores. A Hindu mala has 109 beads, made out of rudraksha (plant) beads, and a Buddhist mala has 108 beads, made out of wood or stone. Using a mala to count your recitations will also be helpful in creating a power item that will help in clearing your mind each time you will wear it around your neck.

Hold the mala in your right hand and count with your thumb or major finger. Do not touch your mala with the index while reciting the mantra, because it would decharge the mala. The process would work within you, and the training would not be in vain at all, but you would not be creating a power item at the same time. This also means that if your mala ever breaks (hope not!) you don't lose all the mantra processes you have done, but you simply lose your power item. Store your mala in a place you consider private, or even better, a place you consider to be sacred. While it would not be dramatic, no one else than your self should touch your mala, to prevent the weakening of your power item.

In case you do not have a mala, we will also provide the recommended time of recitation. The more you recite the mantras, the more effect they have in your mind.

Sanskrit mantra to clear the mind:

Om Shanti Shanti Shanti

Means: Divine Peace Peace Peace

Visualization: everything starts as light blue, fades softly, and eventually, no more visualization at all.

The mantra alone will have a soothing effect to calm your mind, but will not be as efficient until you "connect" to the consciousness it represents. When you first learn this technique, you should use the mantra intensively enough to break the mental limits of non-thought. You must recite the peace mantra for 9 malas or 45 minutes, each day for twelve straight days. We call this "connecting" the mantra. When you practice this technique intensively, you charge your soul with the energy and consciousness invoked by the mantra. Failure to do the 12 days in a row or to recite the appropriate number of malas will result in poor connection and less efficient effects for the remainder of the entire training. If you have difficulties being constant, here is the time to practice. If you miss one day, start the entire process from scratch. For your practice to count, you have to do your process once per 24 hour period, before the sun rises. (I remember coming back from a class, at 2:00 AM, and sitting down to make my japa of the day. I kept falling asleep, so I did it walking around in my meditation room to prevent myself from falling asleep.)

Chanting a mala means you chant 108 mantras. We do not count the 109th bead in the Hindu mala, that is used only once at the beginning to make a prayer, depending on your faith. It could be a prayer to your higher-self asking for more efficient ESP. Chanting 9 malas in a row (972 mantras) for twelve days in a row (11664 mantras) will make the mantra extremely efficient when afterwards you wish to use it for only a few minutes. Chant the mantras while visualizing everything as a clear blue sky. If thoughts come by, let them be softly, and try to pay attention only to the mantra and the clear blue light. It is possible that images NOT originating from your mind will come, but don't pay attention to those either; not yet. When you do japa (recite mantra using your mala) we must pay attention to the philosophical concept that the mantra represents. You may rock your body gently while charging your mantra.

Once you have connected to this mantra's consciousness, if your mind is going crazy or is too filled with thoughts, recite one mala, or 5 minutes of this mantra, while clearing your mind. It is recommended to do one mala of the mantra of peace before each one of your other training practices, except the techniques where you fall asleep.

Meditation

Unlike what we see in commercial meditation, true meditation has to be done in silence, physically and in the mind. Sit, breathe a few times, and calm your mind. When your mind is agitated, chant the mantra of peace a few times. When your mind is getting calm, clear out everything and stay in a state of clarity, simply aware that you are aware. We call this state of mind "self-awareness".

Once you get your attention on being aware, even if a few mental ripples come along, place your attention on yourself, as a soul, not a body. Feel your soul, feel what you are inside, pay attention to your consciousness, your spirit. This part of meditation is simply unexplainable. Just do it. Try to be what you are, without effort. Simply pay attention to what you feel you are, whether you know or not what you are. You are the Self, so be the inner supreme consciousness of the Self.

When your mind takes too much place, go back to chanting the mantra of peace silently, a few times. Then, go back to being the inner Self. This is the source of your real power. Practice this meditation of the Self every day for 2 to 5 minutes.

This technique is so simple that we tend to complicate it. We seek what to feel. We wonder if we are doing it correctly. We doubt, we wander off, we imagine things. This technique is so simple, just do it. Sit, relax, pay attention on nothing, as yourself, with no definition. Don't think of what you are. Don't let thoughts about yourself whirl around in your mind. Don't think. Just be. If you don't know who or what you are, then you are close to the goal.

When you meditate, or when you are doing your japa processes, it is possible that you "transcend". It might look like if you lost consciousness, or went to sleep, but in fact, it is your consciousness that is awakening, and at first, this shuts down the human self for short periods. This is the goal of every technique of transcendental meditation. In a transcendent state of consciousness, you are fully free of your human limitations. You are cleansing your soul, expanding, refilling with light and pure thought.

If you start to snore, or if your body becomes so loose that it can't hold itself up anymore, then you went to sleep. This is not too bad, but it is not the goal of meditation. While seated, if your body can still stand on its own with only your head bowing forward, then you are transcending. If you transcended for too long, your head leaning in front for a while, your neck will be sore and you have to carefully help your head back up with your hands, so that you do not develop neck aches.

The goal of meditation is to empower your Self so much that your spiritual consciousness overrides your human identity for a short moment. When this happens for 200-300 times, after years of practice, a time will come when you will transcend, but remain conscious of what is going on even in a state of expanded consciousness. When you return to your normal state of consciousness, you will also retain from partial to full memory of what happened to you during your transcendental experience.

The reason why our human self passes out is that the level of energy and information at the spiritual level of True Self is so intense that the human cannot withstand it. When we come back from a transcendental state, we know that something happened. Sometimes we feel refreshed, filled with new energy, but other times, we remain dizzy for a moment. Once you come back from this higher state of consciousness, you remain in a state of empowerment and you should only pay attention to good and positive thoughts for at least 20 minutes. Before you become a true adept at meditation, become an adept at controlling your thoughts. You don't want to manifest bad things, and you do want to encourage the manifestation of good events. You are encouraged to repeat to yourself a nice positive thought when you are back from meditation. Repeat mentally a phrase that will encourage your training (My consciousness expands, my mind is pure) or that will promote your general wellbeing (My life is simple, and I am happy).

You should practice meditation at least 5 minutes every day, before or after any other type of spiritual training. On a weekly basis, you should have a meditation period of more then 20 minutes, until you get to the Siddhi path, at the end of this training.

Awaking the Diaphane

The imagination is not just the place of conscious dreaming. The imagination is an organ of the mind able to emit thought-forms and perceive them. Imagination is a multi-dimensional membrane in the mind (like in 3D, but with more dimensions that we can't yet figure out). Membranes are usually 2 dimensional, so use your imagination to grasp what a 3D membrane would be. If you are thinking of a drape floating in the air, you are not dimentionalizing enough. Think about it as an organ with screen-like properties. We will refer to this organ as the "diaphane". Once you become aware of the "diaphane membrane", or the mind-organ of thought-form communication, then we can go on to the next step of the training. A side-effect of this training will be the possibility for having visions. Why train to have visions when you can train in awakening the core of the super-conscious mind that will result in having visions... and much more?!

First step: adding functionality. We already have the ability to emit and perceive, thru our diaphane. We simply let it go to sleep, often by saying "it's just my imagination" or "I had a waked dream", when actual thoughts were actively transmitted or perceived.

Preparation: take a few minutes of paying attention to a relaxed breathing. Breathe softly, and pay attention to it. Clear your mind as much as you can, but let the random thoughts be as they wish; they are coming out. This is a positive mind cleansing process.

Part 1: In your mind, define and isolate a simple thought that will act like a radio tuner. For this purpose, use the thought of a spiritual symbol. Pick any simple symbol of your choice. If you have no idea, use a Christian cross, a Hindu swastika, or the outline of a Buddha. Actively think the thought, and "imagine" your mind radiating the thought form in every direction. (I did not say BRAIN, but MIND. Your entire nervous system, and a bit beyond, must emit). Do not emit with effort, but with relaxed willpower. This means that you must want it a lot, to emit with willpower, but keeping your body relaxed. Emit the symbol of your choice in a light manner, with the color of your choice. This will send the thought form in the universe. You will be making a call.

Part 2: After 2 minutes of emitting, shut your mind and internally listen, feel, look (eyes closed), forget about everything and pay attention to the mind-organ diaphane, not to your physical senses. When thoughts come, let them be, but don't care about them. Putting effort in trying not to think will prevent you from going on. Your thoughts need to come out like crazy at first, until your mind naturally becomes free. With time, or with luck, your mind will settle down. Pay attention and perceive the information / wisdom / knowledge / experience that could come back to you. Someone/something might actually answer your phone call, because it is in the nature of your Spirit to answer willingly.

Alternate between emitting and perceiving, spending an average of 2 minutes per period at first. Then, shorten the emitting and perceiving periods. When you become an adept at this, you will be simultaneously emitting and perceiving. After a 10 to 30 minute period of practice, meditate like you usually do. You might have clear results after one week, or one month of daily practice, but the out-of-focus results should be experienced right from the first few days. Yet, if you have no result after the first five minutes of practice, please don't ask yourself what went wrong. Practice and practice again.

It is acceptable to proceed to the next step of the training before you get any efficient results with the diaphane, but in this case, don't be too hard on yourself if the results take time to show up. The entire ESP training takes time and dedication.

The Body and the Soul

In this next step, we must learn how to pay attention properly. We will do so by awakening our inner awareness of our body, operating two trainings at once.

Our attention usually wavers from one subject to another, rocked by the wind of our thoughts, without our conscious intervention. Even while we watch a movie, we think that we are paying attention to the same thing for two hours in a row, while in fact, the movie is continuously sending in new scenes and sounds, to keep our attention flowing with the story. Or else, we would not even be able to concentrate on the movie. We are unacquainted with paying attention to the same thing for more than a few seconds. If there is not change, if there doesn't seem to be movement, sounds or variations, our mind will try to pay attention to something else, hoping to be stimulated.

On another note (even a completely different subject), we are not used to knowing exactly where we exist. We assume that we exist in our body, but we are not really aware of that fact. We take it for granted and our ability to exist in our body fades away. Some people are not even in their body. We could see them hovering here and there, around their bodies, or partially in contact with it.

During this exercise, we will simultaneously practice ourselves at paying attention, and consciously existing in our body. Hence, we will pay attention to our body. You will have to do this exercise sometimes while sitting on a chair, lying down, or sitting in meditation, cross-legged. The environment, as usual, must be peaceful; not even music. We don't want your mind to be distracted during this exercise. It would only make you believe that you are paying attention, while, in fact, you are constantly entertained by the music. If a sense of panic settles in, it means you are on the right track. At first, the mind will be unsettled at focusing consciously on a single thing without other distractions. Again, let your polluting thoughts go free while your mind is cleaning up, and pay attention to the exercise.

Sometimes, by reflex of conditioning, we approach a technique thinking that we are a body, and that we have a mind, and a soul. It is the other way around. We are a soul, and we have a mind and a body. It is a question of self-identification. While we endure the program in our cells that tells us we are the body, we will never be able to look at the world from another point of view than from our physical eyes. In order to become aware of your body, you must also entrain yourself in remembering that you are not the body, and that you are paying attention to it, like to an exterior object, even though you are within it, as a soul. For a moment, there might seem to be a duality of opinions while your mind changes its point of view. You must remain aware of this unsettling feeling, without pushing it away.

Step 1: Feel your body. Become aware of your body. Make contact with your body using your mind. Awaken to every physical sensation of the body. Be at peace. Relax and keep paying attention. It is like a closed-eye meditation on the physical body. After you feel you have a good connection with your physical body, start repeating to yourself "I am not the body, I am the Soul", over and over again, in a very calm manner. Keep paying attention. Do this technique many times, for periods of 10 to 30 minutes. It is totally acceptable for you to transcend, pass out or fall asleep. Gently but certainly, repeat to yourself "I am not the body, I am the Soul,… I am not the body, I am the Soul,…". Technically, the body is a part of the soul. Yet, when you say to yourself "the body is a part of the soul, thus, I am the body", you are still identifying yourself to the limited physical envelope of the soul. We wish to destroy this belief, and we do so by saying "I am not the body, I am the Soul". Hence, your body is a part of you, but it is not entirely you. You are a Soul.

Step 2: When you succeed in feeling your body like if you were living into it, do the same technique as in step 1, but without the phrase. Simply keep your attention on your body, knowing you are something greater, but don't use words. Try to identify the un-worded pure thought of this abstract concept. When we use words, pure thought becomes human thought. We want to become aware of the difference between human and pure thought; to grasp concepts without the words that describe them. You may want to use the phrase "I am not the body, I am the Soul" a few times at the start of the practice, then elevate the attention to the pure un-worded thought. During that same time, you are also paying attention to your body.

Once you grasp the concept of this practice. Use the Sanskrit mantra that means "I am not the body, I am the soul". The mantra is: **Ma Dehane Me Atma Om**. This mantra is charged with a mala during the Atma Yoga process, which is not the scope of this book. Thus, practice this mantra when going to bed, or when doing a lying down meditation.

This might seem to be difficult when you read the technique, but it becomes clear after a few hours of non-linear practice. After a while, you might feel yourself as a living being inside your body. It might trigger a soothing emotional response from your sensitive body. You might have stuff projected on your mind's diaphane. Accept the presence of these other events, but keep your attention to the main purpose of being the soul in the body, without human thoughts.

The answer to most of your questions is: practice makes perfect. Most questions persist because the experience of altered consciousness did not happen yet. Thus, practice, and give yourself time.

Practicing this technique will: have you re-enter your body if you were out, have you become aware of your soul, have you become aware of your human thoughts and spiritual thoughts, practice your concentration on a simple unmoving concept while your mind cleanses out. This technique is actually very healthy for your body and your mind.

Stay fixed as much as you can on the base thought, feeling and concept "I am not the body, I am the Soul". But while you use your will to stay focused, you must also relax and passively pay attention, without implicating yourself against the disturbances of the mind.

Extra-sensory perception means that perception is occurring beyond the senses. This also means that it is not your body perceiving, but something else of a more subtle nature. The only way to develop these special abilities is to awaken the spiritual bodies, starting by awakening your Self at the level of the Soul.

You may proceed to the next step of the training whenever you feel like it. Be gentle with yourself. You will have results with practice. You will have to go over each step of the training many times before you get tangible results in each of these exercises.

It is recommended to fall asleep each night while saying to yourself "I am not the body, I am the Soul", or the equivalent Sanskrit mantra. The effect of this training will also work at night, during your sleep. Falling asleep while focusing on your Self as the Soul will also have great benefits while you sleep. For some people, this is where they have their first conscious experience of the diaphane when they wake up. But for this to happen they also trained during the day, when awake.

Expanding Consciousness

Meditate on the Self for 2 minutes. Then, imagine your Self having about the shape of your body, and try to feel your spiritual Self inside your body, in a higher vibration level, a higher energy field. You can feel something like a presence in your body.

Once you feel the energy, or the feeling of your Self, start to expand. If you can't yet feel your Self yet, use your imagination. It is not only your energy that expands, but your Self, which is what you are. Imagine your spiritual body becoming bigger than your physical body. Expand your consciousness a few feet beyond your physical body. Then, remain in this state of expansion for a few minutes.

We are used to looking at the world from behind our physical eyes. So much, that when our eyes are closed, we believe we can't see anymore. This is an illusion made from the objective and Cartesian mind. Once you have expanded your consciousness, place your point of view anywhere close to your body, but not from behind your eyes, like you are used to. Look at the surroundings using your consciousness, from various points of views. Go slowly about it. Use your imagination, but let your diaphane also reveal what it sees.

Expand your consciousness, expand your spiritual body, and displace your point of view. Do this for a few minutes each day, until you become efficient at it. Most people want to go too fast, to look in another room, and travel. Do NOT do this yet. When you go too fast and too far, your mind will make up for the missing information. If you notice that what you saw was imagined and not really perceived with consciousness, you will program your mind that "it doesn't really work", and we don't want to produce this kind of negative thoughts. You first have to train yourself at expanding your consciousness, and building the links between your spiritual Self (not limited by your physical body), and your other mental functions, like memory and perception.

Keep on practicing until you develop an awareness of your sensitive body. The diaphane is a part of this sensitive body. Techniques that allow you to move your point of view anywhere you wish will be available in the Siddhi chaper, near the end of the book. You need to be prepared in order to be efficient with the Siddhi path, and develop more powerful supernatural abilities.

Transmigrating Consciousness, Level 1

We spend most of our life experiencing the world from a single point of view: our head. With some experience on expanding your consciousness all around you, we will now learn how to concentrate the focal point of consciousness.

Sit in front of a bottle or glass of water. Take it and drink a bit of water and pay attention to the energy sensation of the water. If you think you can't feel the energy, then pay attention to its taste, its texture. Return the water in front of you. Do one mala of the mantra of peace.

Now, clear your mind and become your spiritual Self for a minute. Then, open your eyes and focus on the bottle or glass of water. Imagine that you are this water. Don't pay attention to your body anymore, even though you might still have perception of your body senses. Simply pay attention on becoming the water. Take its shape, its texture, and know that you are this water, inside the bottle or glass. Once the contact is made with the eyes focusing, close your eyes and transmigrate your consciousness into the water. Become the water, in your mind, your imagination, and if you allready can, as consciousness, as Self.

Migrating would imply moving your consciousness from your body into the water. Transmigrating is simply being there already. You don't have to move from yourself, but simply lose the focus of your human body, and awaken to existing as the water. Your eyes helped to make the focus, to connect to the reality of the water, and then, with eyes closed, your consciousness becomes the water. It is not only displacing your point of view, but becoming the water itself. Imagine it, and feel it.

Once you are the water, chant the mantra of peace in your mind. Your mind is not in your physical body's head, but wherever is your consciousness. Exist as the water for 1-2 minutes, and vibrate the mantra of peace softly. Of course, this requires that you have previously charged yourself with the mantra of peace (connected the mantra of peace with 11664 recitation, 9 malas a day for 12 days).

Then, open your eyes and look at the water. Note the strange feeling of being in your human body, and being the water, at the same time. Take the water and drink it. Pay attention to the feeling of the water that comes into your body. It is like drinking what you are.

Repeat every day for a few days. This is an efficient way to bless water, and then bless your body with the conscious state of peace. This contributes to a healthy body.

You must NOT transmigrate into someone's body, unless this person is aware of the situation. It is useful for a healer to tap into the sickness to heal it from inside. It is useful for an ESP adept to become an object, but it does not mean you will already be capable of reading the energies of an object. Transmigrate into water for a while. It is required to awaken the ability to tune into something else than your body.

Conscious Perception

For this technique to work, you need to have some results with the diaphane technique, at the beginning. If you did not get some results of a spiritual nature when triggering a spiritual call with your diaphane, the following technique might not be so obvious. But then again, for some few, this is where they get their first results in the entire process. So, stay positive, whatever you do.

Take a rock, any rock. It can be a small rock that you pick up here or there, or it can be a big rock that you step on. Sit in front of the rock, or sit on it if it is big enough. Do a mala of peace, then, relax for a minute.

Touch the rock with your hand, and fix it gently with your eyes. Your eyes help to create the conscious contact. Your hands help create a contact at a more sensible level. In any case, sight and touch are two senses of the physical body that you will use to tap into the consciousness of the rock. We don't want to debate here if the rock is alive or simply matter. One thing for sure, there is some vibration, and some frequency in this rock, organized in a manner that we can consciously perceive it with our diaphane.

First, with your eyes and touch, become the rock. Transmigrate into it. Become the rock. Take as much time as you need to transmigrate and feel yourself as the rock. Even if your body senses keep telling you about being your body, there will be a time when you also know that you are the rock.

Secondly, tune into the rock's story. You know what a "story" is. You understand the concept, even if we use the word "story" to refer to the concept of a story, we can imagine the concept without using the word itself. You will send this "story" concept to the rock, in an interrogative attitude, so to ask the rock to tell you its story, using only the feeling and conceptual thought of asking for its story. And then, immediately shut your thoughts to let the answer come back to you. The rock should throw a whole bunch of images to your diaphane. Most people perceive it as a fast-forward story without clear reference to time and space. In any case, the rock should tell you its story, using its own conceptual thoughts.

There is a debate about if a rock has consciousness, or if it is alive, or if it is only matter that records conscious vibrations passing close to it. It is not in the scope of this training to answer these kinds of questions. What we know, is that when a conscious un-worded thought of "tell me your story" is sent to a rock, it shoots back a ripple of all that happened to it.

Once you have success with a rock, in the mineral world, go up to the vegetal world and ask a plant how it feels. Then, train yourself at conscious perception with a fish, and ask it how it feels. Then, entrain yourself with an animal. The simpler the nervous system of the being, the easier it is to have conscious perception. This is why we start this training with a rock, then with a vegetal organism. If you have difficulties having conscious perception with an animal or a fish, go back to the mineral and vegetal world until you have more tangible experiences. (The Shaman who thaught me this technique practices 3 hours a day for 15 years).

When manipulating objects, we leave small traces of our consciousness into them. The same happens when spending time in a room. The stronger the emotion we feel when manipulating objects, or being in a place, the stronger is the consciousness imprint that we leave. Clairvoyance consists in transmigrating into an object, or addressing the consciousness of a room, so to perceive these imprints left by others. We can use clairvoyance to learn the story of an object, or to extract the imprint left by someone we wish to track down afterwards. Try clairvoyance at different points of your training, to see how you can develop this ability.

Compassion and Peace

Until now, not everyone has experienced some kind of extra-sensory perception or supernatural phenomena. It did not matter up to this point, since the goal is to train and practice as much as you can. Before we continue, you now have to learn how to remain at peace. You will soon learn how to interact with animals and humans, and this can become delicate.

We MUST learn how to be untouched by the mental and emotional state of those with who we interact. We must NOT transmigrate into another human being without previously asking permission, but even when we do have permission, the state of mind and heart of the subject could influence our own mind and emotional situation. Even those who seem to be clean and stable might hide, deep inside, a great deal of turmoil and refrained emotions.

We must be able to produce a state of compassion in our heart, at will, and a state of peace in our mind, at will. This is one of the hardest trainings, and will be troublesome for a few. It all depends on your actual state of mind and emotional situation. In any case, this training, along with Emotional Transmutation, will bring you back to mental sanity and stability, and will relieve your heart of some hidden or obvious pain. It will not shield you from what you are, or hide what is inside you. Rather, it will bring you into an easy step-by-step auto-therapy so you can become aware of what you are, at every level.

The most impressive supernatural abilities can be accomplished only when you have the courage to face what is inside your mind and your heart. When you relieve a mental block or an emotional clog, more spiritual power is released from inside you, making it much easier to perceive the subtle worlds, and even interact with them.

Now, we must charge the mantra of compassion.

Sanskrit mantra of compassion:
Om Mani Padme Hum

Approx. meaning: Divine jewel of consciousness, expressed

Visualization: everything starts as multi-colored light, becomes whiter and whiter, and eventually, everything is white. Then, you can release the visualization.

Before we charge this mantra, let's go over its deeper spiritual signification, so we can keep our mental focus on it.

The mantra of compassion starts with the syllable "Om", which represents the highest level of vibration of the universe. Then, the word "Mani", meaning "jewel", refers to something precious and beautiful. The word "Padme", meaning "lotus", a symbol of consciousness, is this pure feeling or pure thought that we are aware of when we meditate on the Self. Then, all of this is expressed into our tangible experience, thru the "Hum". The mantra of compassion expresses in our heart and mind, the highest and most beautiful feelings and thoughts that exist. They are of such a high nature that it takes some time before we can actually become aware of them. We must entrain our heart to feel compassion, and our mind to think in a compassionate way. When compassion comes into consciousness, nothing can hurt anymore, no conflict can exist. At this point, everything is pure, harmonious, and gently joyful.

By connecting your Self to the mantra of compassion, and charging your Soul with its wonderful power, you will summon in your body extraordinary spiritual energies that will fuel everything else from now on. The nature of compassion is so pure and subtle that it will require you to be patient, and faithful to your training. It has taken a while for everyone to feel it.

To refresh your memory, we must chant, silently or with a soft voice, the mantra of compassion, for 9 malas in a row, each day for 12 days in a row, so to attain the progressive charge of 11664 mantras. Before you start chanting your malas of compassion, it is recommended you do one mala of peace, to set the right mental mood. Then, when you're done, take a few minutes of silent meditation, and pay attention to what you are. When you connect/charge the mantra of compassion, the inner feeling of Self might alter and become more refined, while also becoming more present.

If at any time you feel drowsy, sleepy, or attracted to transcend, let yourself go a bit. Then, keep going on your mala where you were at. Try not to drop you mala if you pass out, or else, you have to start back a few beads, just in case. We don't want to fail a process over such minor details.

Emotional Transmutation

The emotional transmutation technique should not be done excessively at first, but is absolutely required to pursue the training. It can be demanding at first, so just begin by doing it once or twice to get the feel of it. Someday when you feel like exploring your emotional world, you may return to this exercise and practice emotional transmutation more often. You may even wait many years before you perform it regularly. It doesn't really matter right now. Someday, you will feel the need to use this technique. When you do, you will double your efficiency in the field of ESP and supernatural abilities.

When a disturbing experience occurs and you want to resolve it, first take all the necessary physical actions that you must, in order to correct the situation, then you can always work at the emotional level to go thru the entire experience (using consciousness to penetrate the experience and absorb it); by this means you can digest the experience and transform it, thus releasing the need for the experience to manifest physically again and again. This is what some teachers call "the transmutation of karma" or "transcending the human experience". I call this the Transmutation of Emotion.

An emotion is not transmuted by actively wishing it to go away, or trying to get rid of it. Every experience occurs so that you may become aware of it; it is only by consciously becoming aware of the full experience that the emotion will be transmuted and released as a new (higher) experience. We experiment with emotions so that the soul can taste life and so that consciousness can know its own existence. We must not flee from painful or difficult emotions, yet we must not intentionally provoke pain either. This process cannot take place while you listen to the inner voice and its natural fear of feeling pain. You will have to be courageous and go beyond your fear; have faith, release control over the emotional pain and become aware of the emotion without engaging it in any way (not break anything, not hurt anyone, nor yourself).

The Transmutation Technique

Begin the Transmutation Technique by selecting some recent event that you feel guilty about or perhaps some event that left you feeling rejected. You may choose any memory, whether in your recent or remote past, as long as it is not an experience you associate with overwhelming painful emotions of any kind (not for the first attempts). Begin with this problematic but bearable emotion, so you can do the emotional work and still be able to follow along with these three simple steps. Remember that you only need to understand and practice these steps in order to master them.

First step (inner contact): Refresh your memory of the emotion and the situation linked to it. Take a deep breath and feel this emotion without limitation. It is in your belly, within you, and you can feel it more and more. Do not amplify it from your normal stance as the victim of this emotion. Instead, listen to it, feel whatever it brings up for you, taste its flavor, accept its shape and form and how it defines itself (even if that is different than how you were defining it), contemplate it, and hold it within you. Be at peace and relive the emotion for a few breaths, up to one full minute. Be at peace. Later in your training you may perform this with some more powerful emotions. For now, just enjoy peacefully contemplating the positive change you just made.

Rarely, you may feel the need to express an emotion outwardly, in order to release some pressure that seems to be building up. On those rare occasions, (and this is not to be done frequently), simply release what you need to let go of, but never lose control over this experiment. When you are just learning these techniques, it is too easy to revert to victim stance, and to begin amplifying how terrible the situation is. Remember that you are practicing just becoming aware of the emotion. When you are unable to bear the intensity of an emotion, you may release some of the pressure; then just continue on with the process. It is obviously not the goal to keep this emotion trapped inside of you, or buried; rather it is the goal of this exercise to release the hold you have on it. Thus it is perfectly fine to perform the process while expressing some normal human emotion. Simply keep track of the experiment without losing your grip on the process. Breathe into your abdomen throughout the entire process. Do not breathe from your upper torso. Hold the situation that caused the emotion in your mind while you feel the emotion.

Second step (integration): Get inside the emotion and follow wherever it leads you. Breathe deeply and comfortably. As the air flows into your abdomen, your task, as consciousness, is to penetrate the emotion and let it absorb you. Be aware of all the feelings that entering this emotion evokes for you, whether you feel pain or emptiness, coldness or heat, anger or sadness. Get inside of it and become it. The process of Integration requires a conscious fusion of you and the emotion. You are going to allow yourself to be enveloped within the emotion; to be integrated into it. For a few minutes, breathe and accept, breathe and become, breath and feel. Follow the path this emotion leads you on, and you will notice that most of the time, the emotion will be covering another emotion that is buried beneath it.

Every emotion arises into our consciousness because it is linked with some human experience. Use your mind to follow these experiences from the past so that you can remember what happened. You might run thru a few events (while following your emotions), until you come to the first time in your life that you felt that emotion. Stay focused. Do not jump from one thread to another; trace one experience to its root cause, following one thread at a time. As you allow the emotions to exist, without avoiding them or rejecting them, the emotion is freed up, and the energy associated with it ceases to be trapped; the emotion is alive again, emancipated. When you stop blocking it and permit it to BE, your consciousness can understand the profound essence of that emotion.

During the exercise of becoming the emotion, this previously problematic feeling will be re-set to a peaceful, natural state and you will get an abstract but clear understanding of your human experience. You are what you experience, as consciousness, as spirit, as life. Do not rush through your experience of this step. Allow the penetrating fusion to continue for a while, until there is no pain associated with the emotion, only the experience of it. Conscious breathing will also naturally relax your hold on the emotion until it is released. Understand that the emotion will not leave you, it will simply be free to remain inside of you without any of the previous negative associations. Always consciously go beyond your fear of pain; never push away the emotion. With your mind, consolidate the entire experience, which is comprised of all of the life events that made it; breathe and be conscious within that entirety.

The human ego has strong natural defense systems. Many times, the emotion is not blocked all by itself. Instead, the human ego keeps control over it, out of arrogance, vanity, jealousy, and envy, the ego refuses to allow the emotion the right to be resolved, all because of pride. You have to be in charge of this experiment and release the mental hold you keep on your emotion. You simply have to let go.

Third step (liberation): When you feel completely saturated with the emotion you are working on, when your consciousness has transmuted it into a living experience, that emotion (and all the energy that was trapped with it) is freed up. It is not released outside of you, it is available to you again, and all the power and potency of the emotion is alive for you once more. The heavy, dense or contracted energy that was troubling you is released in that it is converted into its essence, and dissolved in your higher consciousness. A good feeling will naturally bubble up from within you. You may feel deeply satisfied, or you may experience a profound state of peace, or you may feel the emancipating joy of freedom. Breathe and allow this new feeling of joy to fill you up, release this positive emotion if you wish to.

After this transmutation, the most important thing for you to do is to contemplate the wholeness of the experience as joyful life and happiness. Even if your physical human experience did not seem to change at all, your inner experience of it became one with the inner Self. Do not let your human ego steal this moment from you. It is crucial for you to rejoice within yourself, for you have tasted life at its fullest.

Sample Application

A few days before I began writing this book, I was struck with insecurity. I did a bit of Kuji-In (spiritual practice I like), breathing in while focusing a bit on the fire visualization (also part of Kuji-In) but mostly concentrating on the philosophy that "Life takes care of me, I am not alone, God is with me, and I trust life". I allowed myself to release my control over that feeling. I stopped the Kuji-In practice so I could concentrate on emotional transmutation.

At each in-breath, I let myself feel the emotion, completely aware of it, allowing myself to feel every sensation that came up, and to absorb the 'flavor' of these feelings. In order to get underneath the fear, I went down to the emotion of feeling abandoned. I sat within the emotion of abandonment in a state of complete acceptance for some time. I felt sad about the abandonment. It took a few minutes before I got to the depth of my sadness. My goal was to be conscious of it, without struggling against it, or trying to change it. I followed the experience deeper, and deeper, only to discover that I was afraid of not having enough money. In my early 20's I experimented with being a beggar. Each day I hoped to eat, and I came to believe that life was very hard. A few minutes later, after I had questioned myself more and more extensively as to why I had to go through the experience of being a beggar, I sought to remember some time in the more distant past when I had felt this same emotion. I remembered my brother stealing my toys and I suddenly realized *that* was when I started believing life would not give me what I want.

As I accepted that I have no control over my life, sitting in that knowledge and understanding it for quite a few breaths, the insecurity gradually dissolved and the emotion disappeared. In fact, it did not actually go away; it was transmuted into trust. Thus, I came to understand the entire experience, and the emotion became what I sought, thanks to the wonderful process of evolution.

It can take years of suffering for a normal human being to grasp the essence of a single lesson, and this process is rarely accomplished consciously. This lack of conscious understanding permits the negative events to re-emerge over and over. With conscious integration of an emotional experience, a few hours, sometimes even a few minutes are enough to release the entire experience for you. Sometimes the experience does re-emerge again later, but only to be integrated at another level, and again, only a small amount of time is necessary to transmute it, compared to the natural evolution process. Some people resolve one karmic event every 10 years. Most cannot resolve more than a few lessons in their lifetime. Evolutionary beings can resolve these experiences 'in bulk' every once in a while, each time making their life easier and happier.

I practice Emotional Transmutation almost every day. Sometimes for a few seconds, to become aware of what I feel. Sometimes, I do it for a few minutes, to process an emotion and release it. Once in a while, I take an entire hour to process a full time-space strand of experiences linked to an emotional state. This is a key to power.

Emotional Transmutation Training

Every day, for 12 days, do one mala of peace, one mala of compassion, followed by a few minutes of calm meditation. Then, take one emotion that you experienced in the past, and transmute it. Start by getting into it, like transmigrating into the emotion, like you would with a rock or a glass of water. Sink into your emotion and become it, and follow it until you reach its origins. After some time, between 10 to 30 minutes, or when you've cleared an emotional strand and attained a natural state of joy, sit in a calm contemplative state and be at peace. When you feel ready, do one mala of peace and one mala of compassion.

Transmigrating Consciousness, Level 2

Before you practice the second level of consciousness transmigration, it is absolutely essential that you have charged the mantra of peace, the mantra of compassion, and have trained into emotional transmutation for 12 successful days. If you could not face the music when going down inside you, you will naturally block yourself form success with others. Also, you would not want to have someone else feel your little troubles inside you. You'd still be stuck with them, and you would have uselessly have projected the feeling to someone else.

This training is not required to be 12 straight days, since it requires that you feel good when you do it. If you can't get to a peaceful and compassionate state of consciousness, go again over the previous trainings and clear yourself out. Of course, you don't have to wait to become a saint before you go on the next step of the training. You know when you feel good or bad, stable or not. If you spend most of your life in a state of depression or anguish, skip this technique entirely. It won't destroy your training, it will simply make it different.

On a day that you feel good, or at least peaceful, pick someone you like, that you already have a relationship with.

Don't go picking someone you would like to be in relationship with. This would throw off the focus of the technique. Now is the time to be grateful to your parents, or to a close friend.

Sit down and open up your practice session with the standard mala of peace and mala of compassion. Then, think of the person you chose. Breathe softly and deeply a few times. When you feel you have made contact with the "concept" of this person, that you hold the frequency of this person in your consciousness, transmigrate into his/her body by sitting right into it. Imagine that you are already there, you are this person. You will feel the strange feeling of multiple identities. You will still have a link with your own identity (you can't really lose that), but you will also feel that you are someone else, or at least, in someone else's body.

After one or two minute of focusing on the person's consciousness frequency, or when you feel the combined consciousness of identities, pick up your mala with your own physical body, and do one mala of peace followed by one mala of compassion. All along, keep in mind that you are in someone else's body, and that in consciousness, you are one. You will be elevating the consciousness of someone else, purifying their mind and their heart a bit. It will not be as efficient as if they were doing emotional transmutation on their own, but it will be as efficient as your own ability to transmigrate your consciousness, and your connection experience with each mantra.

When you are done, simply come back to yourself, in your own body. Rest a lot during this training period. Focus your thoughts on joy and happiness. Don't ask the target person if they experienced anything, unless you don't mind being labeled as a freak. Humility recommends that you keep these experiences for yourself unless your target person is opened to these kinds of things.

To put someone else in a certain state of consciousness, you must first be able to produce this effect within yourself. By learning how to heal your body using supernatural ways, you will eventually be able to produce this effect into someone else's body. The same will happen with relieving depression, soothing pain, and many other states of consciousness.

Everything that you do to someone else with this technique comes back to you ten times stronger. I personally experienced this technique when I played with the dark arts in my teens, and I ended up amplifying a few psychological problems of my own. The effects were light negative moments on the target person, and heavy anxiety on me. Wow! Was I stupid! I certainly was not experienced in life. At least it proved to me once again that all these things worked, but I could also have confirmed it using more compassionate means. One of my close students (Jean-Patrick) discovered he had this power by relieving someone of a depressive state, to find out that even this person's environment was happier than usual for a while. Not only was he surprised and happy, but he received joyful benefits in return. I do recommend that every student learns how to produce a state of compassion and peace, at will.

You cannot save anyone by using the transmigration of consciousness. You cannot do emotional transmutation for others, or relieve them of their own karma. All you can do is influence others with a spiritual power, or charged mantra.

It is useful to gain information from someone. Yet, whatever information you gain might be altered by your own imagination projected on your diaphane. The information perceived from others is not the truth. It is what they nourish with their own consciousness. What you perceive this way could be the truth, or their personal made up fantasy. They might not even be aware of it themselves. Do not try to read minds with this techniques; it delivers poor results. This power is mostly useful for therapists and healers, to identify a health situation or find good leads regarding the condition of a patient.

Attention vs. awareness

For the remainder of this training, please assimilate these two concepts: "Paying attention to", and "being conscious of". "Paying attention to" is done at the mental level, where you place your mental focus on something. This is what you do when you use a mantra, visualization or other technique that requires the implication of your mind. "Being conscious of" is not about thoughts, nor mental activity, but about awareness at a more subtle level. This is what you are doing when you transmigrate, or when you perceive using your diaphane.

Paying attention is done with the mind, while being conscious is done with consciousness. You are probably only at the edge of starting to make out the difference between mental thoughts and consciousness. Give yourself time, and practice a lot. In time, you will have more experience of what it is to be conscious, aware at the spiritual level, as a spiritual being. From there, you will start to feel and perceive with consciousness, in a way similar to what you do with your physical senses.

The Supernatural World

Until now, you have learned how to awaken dormant systems of consciousness in you. Each student is at a different place in this training, and each student gets different results. However, the constant is the progressive awakening to the supernatural world. Before we can experience supernatural phenomena, we have to be aware of the supernatural world. Before we can make supernatural actions, we have to be functional in the supernatural world.

Let us define "supernatural" as what is beyond the natural. What is natural is what exists in nature. Thus, what is supernatural is what exists beyond nature. Supernatural abilities do not always take place in the physical realm. Some supernatural activity remains in the supernatural realm and is not observed by un-awakened people. However, the goal of a training program such as this one is to be able to observe in nature phenomenon that originated from beyond nature.

The awakening of your consciousness so far gave you a general idea of what it is to awaken spiritually. Someone is awake physically if the physical body is functioning, if it is alive and aware. Someone is awake emotionally if the person is aware that there are emotions, can identify some of them, and can choose how to deal with them. Do not be fooled, we are not always emotionally awake. Sometimes, we react to an emotion without paying attention to the emotion itself. In such cases, we simply act without thinking, without feeling, according to the programmed response that the body holds for such emotional states. This gives birth to reactions of jealousy, envy, anger, sexual attraction, that apparently, on the moment, we could not control. We then say that "it was stronger than me". This happens because the physical-emotional-mental software is a great creation of nature, and it works perfectly to promote the preservation of the biological body, and then, to preserve the human race. The technique of "Emotional Transmutation" is one of the best ways to awaken the emotional body, and remain in charge of its activities.

Most people are partially awake physically, emotionally, and mentally, but are not awake spiritually. A few people are awake physically, barely awake emotionally, and totally dormant mentally. Even though they seem to have cognitive abilities, these humans only respond to stimuli according to their conditioning, and are not able at all to make a real free-will choice. Their choices are conditioned programs to which they obey. Luckily, if you're undergoing this training, you most certainly are awake mentally. The goal is to awaken even more to the spiritual reality. Only then will you be able to have interactions between the supernatural and natural planes of experience.

It is by remaining awake at the physical, emotional, mental and spiritual level, simultaneously, that we can aspire to be able to produce interactions between these various planes of existence. There is also a plane of existence between the physical and emotional realities, that I like to call the ethereal plane, which is composed of willpower and life energy. This is where the "Chi" is held, and this is the plane that we stimulate to deploy our will. The difference between the ethereal plane and the emotional plane is the same as the difference between desire and want. Will power is energy that wants something, and it promotes actions in the physical plane. Desire is an emotion that does not necessarily go lower in manifested reality. Desire does not always become reality. Desire is the emotion that fuels the amount of willpower that will be deployed in a physical action. This entire process is called by the mind, that tunes into an intention. Intention is a thought.

The following is a simple chart that will help you understand the various planes of existence and their relationship to the generation of physical phenomena, such as an action. These planes are all part of nature. (Constituent = what it is made of. Resultant = what it produces)

Plane	Symbol	Constituent	Resultant
Mental plane	Mind	Thoughts	Intention
Emotional plane	Heart	Emotions	Desire
Ethereal plane	Guts	Life energy	Will
Physical plane	Body	Flesh	Action

Above the natural planes lies the spiritual planes, the Self. It is made of consciousness, soul and spirit. It can produce all forms of phenomena found in nature, such as pure thought, pure intention, pure desire, pure will, and ultimately, pure action.

A properly functioning human can produce efficient actions by simultaneously:
- Concentrating on a specific intention
- Amplifying the force of the action with an honest desire
- Amplifying the force of the action with a strong will
- Producing the desired action with a healthy body

The scope of the next few chapters will be to awaken our awareness of the supernatural world. Only then will we be able to build efficient tools to work between all the planes of existence. The ultimate goal is to reach a range of consciousness and a strong set of tools that will permit our Spirit to product physically observable phenomena, after we have gone thru the required training. But almost immediately (weeks, months) we will be able to experience interactions between the Spirit and the mind (mind reading, spontaneous telepathy…), followed by interactions between the Spirit and the heart (soothing emotional pain, stimulate joy, awareness of other's emotions…). Eventually, the Spirit, the Self, will affect our ethereal body by inflating and supporting our life force. The ultimate spiritual influence is when the entire Self influences the physical body, extending lifespan and regenerating the body at a supernatural rate.

Infinite Light Awakened

Now that we have a good idea of what is going on with consciousness, now that we know there is "something out there", thanks to a few experiences of conscious interactions at the spiritual level, it is time to refine our notion of consciousness and expand beyond the intellectual acceptable standards. We have to bypass the mental conditioning we received since birth. We have to get a much better idea of what is consciousness, of how it works, and how to act with it like we would act in physical reality.

First, let us contemplate what is "Light". Light is not seen, yet we know it is there, since we perceive the objects that the light reflects upon. For us to see physical reality there has to be light everywhere, so that a part would enter our eyes. Light is something inconceivable in itself. We can only consider the experience of its byproducts, the resultant interaction of light with objects. Thus, let us now think of the difference between the "light" itself, and the fact that we perceive. Look around you a bit; look at things. Then, remove your attention from the things you look at, and put your attention on the infinite amount of light everywhere around you, in the air, that flows in every direction. Try to get a grasp of what it could be, not with your mind, but by being conscious of it. It won't be easy at start. The goal is not to become aware of light immediately, but to practice at trying to identify the conscious phenomena of light. You might never even feel light itself, but you will have practiced at expanding into it, and being conscious of its existence.

Take 2 minutes right now, to be aware of light, and not paying attention to objects, while keeping your eyes opened. Take a few relaxing breaths. Expand into light.

Another concept that is hard to grasp with the mind, yet obvious for consciousness, is the concept of the "infinite". Our mental conditioning requires that each thing be calculated, measured, assimilated mentally so that we can attribute it a numerable value according to some conditioned standard, or rule. Our mind wants to encase everything in a box, with a definite dimension, volume, weight, time span… The concept of infinity is only available to our mind at a philosophical level. However, for consciousness, infinity is totally obvious. By awakening our consciousness, we will progressively make these unconceivable concepts available to our minds. We will be able to have thoughts deprived of limits. We will think beyond dimension.

Take 2 minutes, right now, to absorb your mind in "infinity", without limits, forever going in time and space, without possible measurement. Allow your mind to think without definition. Contemplate and breathe.

Contemplating "light" as it is, and "infinity" as it is, was only to give you an idea of what to pay attention to, and be conscious of, when you will do the next technique.

Now that you grasp the concepts of: infinite, light and awakened, let us move on to a new training technique that is called, simply enough: Infinite light awakened.

The Buddha thaught many things to his disciples. One of the most popular traditions in Buddhism is the Pure Land tradition. Although this training is not meant to expose the entire Pure Land teachings, we will consider its main practice. It consists in contemplating, in a meditative state, the Infinite Light Awakened.

In Sanskrit, the words "infinite light" are said "Amitabha". In Sanskrit, the word "awakened" is said "Buddha". When we chant or recite "Amitabha Buddha" for long periods of time, while gently mentally contemplating the concepts of being awakened to the infinite light, we become aware of what we are, in Spirit. We become the Self. The Buddha himself thought that when we chant "Amitabha Buddha" we are not invoking the Buddha, nor any Buddha at all, but contemplating the highest definition of the Self. This mantra is called the Pure Land mantra.

The technique is simple. Sit in meditation and recite the mantra, or chant it aloud if it is appropriate in your environment. While you chant aloud or recite mentally, also keep in mind its signification. Let your mind dwell on the undefined concept of the Self.

For the sake of this training, you may choose between two possible programs:

1) For 12 days in a row, sit silently and recite mentally the Pure Land mantra for 30 minutes, while allowing your body to rock gently. Eyes closed or partially opened.

2) For 12 days in a row, chant the Pure Land mantra aloud for 15 minutes, then meditate on it for another 15 minutes, eyes closed, repeating the mantra mentally.

At first, we do not use a mala to charge this mantra. It is meant for contemplation. You may charge this mala when done with the entire training provided in this book, and seek new mantras that you could charge.

Mother and Father

A father holds his newborn child with joy and gladness. Then he contemplates the beauty of what he created. Sometimes, he will even shout to everyone "This is my child" and think, deep inside "this is what I made, I created this". For a moment, the father is convinced that he made the child, all by himself. And the mother, looking at the baby, simply loves the baby for itself. She does not feel the need to affirm she made the child. It is obvious for her, and she prefers to care for the newborn, as it is her dearest treasure.

In most religions, the man will pray to God as a man. He will pray to the creator, the one who intended creation, the one who desires creation, the one who willed/wanted creation, but who prays to the Divine female energy that actually created it all. In a business, sometimes the head management proudly looking at the manufactured product does not pay attention to the workers and infrastructures required to make the product. You could also notice that employers paying attention to, and caring for their employees will obtain better results form their businesses. Everyone tends to pay tribute to the originator of a creation, and to the resulted creation, but will not care about the entire process of creation situated between the creator and the created.

Whatever your system of belief, whatever the name of your God, if any, you must take time to pay attention to the Divine Mother, the feminine energy of creation.

There is not much to explain here. Those who have success with supernatural abilities are those who have a balanced relationship with both the male and female Divine energies. Most of our spiritual processes are done with the masculine energy as a base, so we must develop a relationship with the feminine Divine energy to re-balance.

From time to time, I like to do a mala with this simple mantra: "Divine Mother, I love you and I receive your love". This is my way of connecting to the Divine Mother. You should try it and see what comes up. The Buddhists can pray to the goddess Tara. The Hindu can pray to the goddess Durga. The Christians can pray to the Holy Mother Maria.

Pranayama

There are a great deal of breathing exercises of many different styles. Every serious spiritual path encourages adequate breathing. Here we will cover one specific type of breathing exercise that fills your energy system and blows on the fire dormant in your base chakra.

Prana is life energy. When you breathe, you not only take in oxygen, but prana. Prana will naturally circulate in your energy system. If you wish to consciously use prana to direct it as you wish, you must practice pranayama often.

The pranayama technique is more complicated than most breathing techniques. Before we go with the pranayama, let's take a look at our breathing pattern. Place your right hand on your upper chest, and your left hand on your abdomen. Take a deep abdominal breath, then slowly let go. If your right (upper) hand moved, then you are not breathing correctly. During pranayama, in fact during any breathing, you should breathe from your abdomen, and not your upper chest. Your upper chest will always move a little, but your abdomen should be doing most of the movement. Practice a few slow abdominal breaths, to develop the reflex.

Physical technique

Leave your left hand resting on your lap, palm up, doing the "fire circulation" mudra, gently touching the tip of your index finger to the tip of your thumb. Do not place your thumb above the index nail, but touch the tip of the fingers. This will allow more circulation of prana in your system.

With your right hand, gently touch the tip of your right index to your tongue, so to humidify it just a tiny bit. Then, put your right index on your third eye, between your brows. Don't push, simply touch. Keep your eyes closed.

Alternation breathing:

1- Using your right major, block your left nostril. Breathe in thru your right nostril. Hold the breath up for a few seconds.

2- Unblock your left nostril, and block your right nostril with your thumb. Breathe out slowly thru your left nostril. At the end of the breath, stay fixed for a few seconds.

3- Keeping your right nostril blocked with your thumb, breathe in thru your left nostril. Hold the breath up for a few seconds.

4- Unblock your right nostril, and block your left nostril with your major. Breathe out thru your right nostril

Using this alternation breathing, you will breathe in thru your right nostril, breathe out thru your left, breathe in thru your left, and breathe out thru your right nostril, each time taking a short pause at the end of each inhale and exhale.

Do the alternation breathing now, 3 times, simply to get used to the physical technique.

TIP: Sometimes, I have trouble breathing in and out because of partially blocked nostrils. When I block my left nostril with my major, I use my thumb to pull my right upper cheek skin a bit, so to relieve pressure in my right nostril. When I block my right nostril with my thumb, I use my major to pull my left upper cheek.

TIP: Blow your nose before your pranayama practice. If you are sick and your nose is clogged, either postpone your pranayama, or do only 3 breath alternations, even if it is hard.

Mental technique

While the breath goes up a nostril and down the other, the mind will be busy with a completely different set of thoughts. During your breath in from the right nostril, your attention will describe a path like so: from your right lung, up your right bronchia, into your throat, up your head, and end 2 inches above your head when your breath in reaches its end. While you keep your breath in for a few seconds, keep your attention above your head. Energy will naturally follow this attention path. Don't visualize too much, nor try to move the energy yourself. Simply follow the path with your attention.

When you start to breathe out thru your left nostril, your attention will go back down into your head, down your throat, down to your left bronchia and your left lung. Leave your attention in your left lung while your breath is stopped.

Then, do the inverse process while following your breathing pattern. As you breathe in thru your left nostril, your attention will follow up your left bronchia, up your throat, up your head and end above your head, where you pause for a few seconds. Then, breathing out thru your right nostril, bring your attention back down your head, down your throat, to your right bronchia and pause in your right lung.

There will be some confusion if you think about the air pattern. If you think to yourself that when you breathe in your right nostril, air goes down in your right lung, then you will be confused with the attention pattern, that is going up with your breathe in. The attention pattern does not follow the movement of the air in your body. While you breathe in, move your attention up on the side of the breathing in nostril, and when you breathe out, move your attention down into your lung, on the side of the breathing out nostril.

Let's add the final touch to the mental process. During the entire pranayama practice, recite the short mantra "OM", one about every one or two seconds. Whether you breathe in, out, or at a pause, your mind is continually going with a soft "OM, OM, OM, OM, OM…".

Review of the technique

Physically, you are breathing in thru a nostril, pausing, and breathing out the other. Then you alternate directions. Mentally, your are following a path with your attention, from your lung on the same side of the inhale, up to above your head, pause, then down to your lung on the same side as the exhale. All along, you softly recite short "OM, OM, OM…" in your mind.

Start with 1 minute of pranayama, and increase each day one minute at a time, until you reach an average of 15 minutes. If your eyes get sore, or if the inside of your nose burns, stop immediately. Keep your spine erected but relaxed, during the entire practice.

Once or a few times, you might try pranayama for 30 or even 45 minutes, to give a great prana surge into your energy system. This will train your energy system at gathering more energy. It will also work on awakening your kundalini.

Kundalini is a very powerful force strongly tied in our base chakra. When we first awaken the kundalini, it is not the kundalini itself that we feel, but vapors of energy released from the base chakra, that travel along the spine, and on each side of the spine. When the kundalini completely awakens and rises to the brain, we become a divine being walking on earth. Don't be so pressed into saying you have awakened your kundalini.

When we do pranayama, the air circulates according to the natural pattern, into the lungs. The attention goes another way, and we recite a short mantra. But the prana also works in yet another way, stimulating energy channels along the spine. Some of the prana goes down along the spine, to the base chakra, and blows on the fire of kundalini to awaken it.

The technique of pranayama is an essential component of every other technique that follows. It is essential that you re-read this chapter and develop an expertise at practicing pranayama.

Power Enhancement

Supernatural abilities are all based on our capacity to influence nature with our Spirit. First, we learned how to perceive the spiritual world and the different planes of existence, so that we could see what we were doing. This being partially done, we will now work at building tools to work with consciousness. From here on, we will go beyond passive perception, and into active manifestation.

Spiritual tools are made with various energies, molded by consciousness. Some tools act on the mental plane, and are made out of pure thoughts. Other tools will act on the emotional plane, and are made out of conscious emotions. To influence the vital plane, intense energy tools are required. But to influence the physical plane, we do not wish to use physical tools, since this would not be supernatural anymore. To influence the physical plane in a supernatural way, we must build tools that exist at every other level, crossing the vital, emotional and mental plane, up to consciousness.

To continue on the path of supernatural abilities, we need to empower ourselves with the raw matter that will permit us to build these tools. Charging ourselves with these energies will also constitute basic tools.

The 5 Elements

The five elements are more than the tangible elements we think of when we speak of earth, fire, spirit, water and air. The spiritual five elements refer to their concept, rather than their physical manifestation. We will explain the concepts to contemplate while you charge the mantras of the five elements. The following concepts are what I like to refer to the basic five elements, where we go to the core of their energy. For each of the five elements, you will do a 9 x 12 type charge, reciting 9 malas, or 35 minutes, each day for 12 days. Using a mala goes a bit faster than 35 minutes, when you are used to the spelling of the mantras.

Each of the five elements mantras call forth the assistance of Divine concepts that most people refer to as gods. We do not believe that there are actual human people in the personal forms of Bhumidevi, Agni, Shiva, Durga, Hanuman... These are the representation of the highest forces acting in the universe, and these mantras use the Hindu and Buddhist approach to invoking their intervention. There are no real elemental processes that do not invoke the help of the Divine forces. However, everyone may call upon the Divine names of their own system of belief. We will provide an explanation of each mantra, and offer variation possibilities, for the student to call the Divine forces using the names that corresponds to their system of belief.

Many traditions have classified the five elements in different ways. They all have ways of associating fingers with each of their elements, and all are good. We recommend you only learn one system of finger/element combination, but using two is also acceptable, if you can mentally switch from one to the other without confusion. The Kuji-In (Japanese Vajrayana Buddhist practice) uses the Japanese finger/element system, while here, we'll use the Hindu/Original Buddhist system. While using a technique, use the finger system associated with it, and change your finger system when you change to a technique that was built using another system.

As a simple example, the thumb is the Void element in the Japanese system, and the Earth element in the Hindu system. But both are said to bring mental health. The Japanese associate Air to the index, and the Hindu associate Fire to the index finger. But both are used to describe the expression of power. Keep an open mind when dealing with various methods of different origins. They all have their efficiency, or else, they would not have lasted thru the ages.

The Japanese Buddhists classified the elements according to their density: solid (earth), liquid (water), gaseous (air), igneous (fire) and pure energy (void). The Chinese saw the elements according to their usefulness in creating other things. Since air is not used to create anything, it is not present in the Chinese elements: earth, wood, fire, metal, water.

The Hindu and original Buddhists saw the elements in their spiritual concepts: generation (earth), elevation (fire), summit of existence (heavens), flow (water), and expansion (Air). The Hindu elements are the most spiritual, conceptual, abstract and hard to understand of all the elemental systems. This is why we will use this system to train in the five elements, since it also delivers the most powerful and immediate effects, because it invokes the presence of the Divine forces. It is the only system that affirms the dependence of the creation to its creator. We will also use this Hindu / Buddhist finger system.

Thumb: earth
Index: fire
Major: heavens
Ring: water
Pinky: air

A student once asked me if it was acceptable to charge more than one mantra at a time, and if he could use another finger system to charge the Hindu elemental mantras. He had been training for years in the ninjutsu finger system. This is what I answered to him:

About charging more than one mantra at a time, you may, while following a simple rule. When charging mantras from series (like the elements) you have to be certain to start the mantra charges in order to finish charging each mantra before you finish the next one following it. Start the fire mantra charge after you start the earth mantra charge, so that you finish the fire charge after you finish the earth charge. This also means that if you charge the earth and fire elements in the same twelve days, you simply have to do the earth mantra first, and the fire mantra charge next. The same goes for charging Kuji-In mantras (not doing the Kuji-In mudra while you hold you mala). We don't charge the mantras of the Siddhis, found later in this book.

As for the finger systems, there are about 20 different finger/element classifications systems, different from one another, depending on the tradition. One is not better than another. When you use 2 esoteric systems that use 2 different finger systems, here are a few options:

- You have to learn both if you wish to use both in the future for healing purposes. You have to use both from time to time, to keep both alive, and mentally switch to the required system when needed.

OR

- If you accept that you will be using the Hindu system mantras only to charge your energy system and do the work internally, you may use the finger system of your choice.

OR

- If you ever wish to use the elements Hindu mantras to heal others, you have to re-charge with the Hindu system fingers if you previously charged using another finger system

OR

- Not use any fingers, but the entire palm of the hand, while you treat the people using the Hindu elements mantras. It is a bit less efficient, but might avoid you the confusion if you don't want to handle multiple finger/energy systems.

OR

- Charge the Hindu elements mantras using your preferred finger system, and remember to use the finger you have associated to each element when you will learn how to heal using the Hindu elemental mantras. This will also diminish the amplitude slightly.

To avoid all this confusion, we usually say that you should re-learn a new system, and switch mentally when needed, but if you are able to cope with it, use the system you like. However, the most efficient way to heal or work with the Hindu mantras, is to use the Hindu finger system previously charged that way. From there, make your own choice.

The most important part of all these techniques is the energy invoked, the mental attitude and the attention directed with consciousness. Now that you know all this, you understand better how to deal with all those finger/energy systems. I personally learned two systems: the Japanese Vajrayana system, and the Hindu elemental system. However, most of my students prefer handling only one system at a time. Make your own choice and deal with it in the future. If you ever learn the Hindu elemental healing technique, you'll have to translate each finger I mention to the finger system you charged.

Now, let us move to the Hindu elemental mantra system.

Earth

Most people will think of earth as a symbol of stability, while the spiritual concept of earth is generation. Stability is linked mostly to the symbol of a rock, which is a part of the earth element. From the earth comes out life and it contains all the metals that manage electro-magnetic fields. Earth does encompass the concept of stability, but it goes so much further. The earth element is the most important element to keep elevated in your energy system. It is the base of creation, and it is also the base of mental health. Have you ever seen a "down-to-earth" person with mental illness? Most mentally ill people are not connected to the earth element.

While you charge the earth element, or simply recite the mantra, think of the life giving aspect, the generation of plants, and the support of electro-magnetic fields. The earth element will stabilize and purify your Chi, your life energy. It will support protection circles around you, at the physical and spiritual levels.

The earth mantra: Om prithividhatu Bhumideviya

Om: Divine syllable

Prithivi: earth, the dirt

Dhatu: nature of, aspect of

Bhum: earth, the planet

Devi: divinity

Ya: grammatical association

The earth mantra invokes the energy of the earthly nature of the divine being that is our planet. All traditions may recite this mantra and respect their tradition. The English translation would be something like "earthly nature of the goddess Earth".

Once you have charged the earth mantra, you will be able to invoke protection energies each time you recite the mantra mentally or aloud. Your mental health will increase. Your paranoia will disappear. Your Chi / Life force will flow harmoniously in your body. The earth element is an essential before we can proceed to other trainings that involve interaction with the material world.

The earth mudra: If sitting, gently turn your left hand into a relaxed fist, and gently touch the ground with the tip of your thumb. Do the same with the right hand if you are not holding a mala. If standing, do the same mudra, turning your fist to point your thumb downwards. This will accentuate your contact with the earth.

Enhanced charge: if you wish to charge the earth mantra with more intensity, put your left thumb into a small bowl of black gardening dirt while you charge the mantra. If you can do it outside without being disturbed, put your left thumb directly in the ground.

Fire

The fire element is NOT the concept of burning and destruction, although it can be used for such applications, mostly in purification processes. The fire element's true form is not destructive. Fire takes matter from a certain level of vibration, and it brings it to another higher level. Fire elevates the energies. It purifies the dense stagnant energies and transforms them in a higher nature, unclogging your energy circuitry. Fire also brings change and renewal.

In nature, we can observe how fire will transform solid compounds into liquid or gaseous forms. It alters the molecular structure and the chemical formulation of components. Fire generates energy, and makes every other process powerful.

While you use the fire mantra, contemplate the power generating forces, and the elevating effect.

The fire mantra: Om Tejasdhatu Agnaya

Om: Divine syllable

Tejas: Power, energy, force associated to fire

Dhatu: nature of, aspect of

Agni: Fire, both the form and Divinity (Agnaya here)

Ya: grammatical association

Agni is not a Divinity limited to any tradition. It is more popular in the Hindu tradition, but it simply means fire, in the form of an intelligent natural force. Fire is the most powerful force in nature. This mantra means something like "Powerful nature of Fire". In sanskrit, sometimes we write the word Fire using "tejas" and sometimes using "agni".

The fire mudra: rest your hand on your knee or lap, palm up. Touch the tip of the index to the tip of your thumb. Do it with your left hand if using a mala, or with both hands otherwise.

Enhanced charge: Fix a flame with your eyes, or the image of a flame, or a symbol of fire, during the entire charge, while trying to blink as little as possible.

Heaven

The heaven element is of the highest spiritual nature. It invokes the action of God in your life. It is the spiritual element. It is the tool of all spiritual activity. Charging this mantra elevates your consciousness. If you are not already born (fully existing) in the spiritual realm, this mantra will accelerate the process.

The Heaven mantra: Om Akashadhatu Shivaya

Om: Divine syllable
Akahsa: Heavens, spiritual realms
Dhatu: nature of, aspect of
Shiva: Lord Shiva, third person of the Hindu trinity
Ya: grammatical association

Shiva is the third personalized concept of the Holy trinity. Where the Christians name the "Father, Christ, Holy Spirit", the Hindu name the "Bramha, Vishnu, Shiva". The Buddhist would see the trinity of their concepts in "Amitabha, Mahastamaprapta, Avalokiteshwara".

If you feel uncomfortable praying to Shiva using the original Hindu mantra, you can recite the mantra using the name of the Christian Holy Spirit/Ghost said in Sanskrit like so: Om Akashadhatu Baghavaatman

Or using the equivalent of Shiva in the Buddhist tradition: Om Akashadhatu Avalokiteshwara

The heaven mudra: touch the tip of your major with the tip of your thumb.

Enhanced charge: Gently look upwards with your eyes, while charging this mantra. You can also contemplate a spiritual symbol, or the statue of your God.

Water

In water, life is born. Water is the supporting substance in which all life dwells. Water fashions earth. Water is the element that represents the womb of the universe. All is within a form of water of a higher nature that encompasses, penetrates and pervades the entire universe. There is no matter that exists without this primeval water. It is the infinite light of creation, in a tangible form. It is the base constituent of Chi and life force.

The water process connects you with life, movement, and the universe. It is in this primeval water that we extend our consciousness. Charging the water mantra connects us to the flow of life. It purifies our body, heart and mind. It soothes our aches, it cares for us.

The water mantra: Om Apsadhatu Durgaya

Om: Divine syllable
Apsa: water
Dhatu: nature of, aspect of
Durga: Divine mother, consort of Shiva, Hindu tradition
Ya: grammatical association

The name Durga(ya) can be changed to the Christian name of the Divine mother, Maria(ya), or the Buddhist name Tara(ya).

The water mudra: touch the tip of the ring finger to the tip of the thumb.

Enhanced charge: Place your left hand in a bowl of fresh water, or do the charging process while in a bath.

Once you have charged the water mantra, the effects will become available naturally. Your level of energy (life) will increase. Your heart will be more stable, while your mind will become more flexible. Charging the water mantra gives your healing ability a great boost. It supports all manifestations.

Air

It is thru air that information is shared, and movement takes place. Air supports all kinds of vibration while altering them the least. Air lets light thru. The air is where sounds travel. The air mantra opens your mind and other senses to information. It helps you perceive in every way. It also takes part in any kind of traveling and motion. The air mantra will also free your mind from limiting thoughts. It will broaden your perception of the universe and of yourself.

The Air mantra: Om Vayudhatu Hanumantaya

Om: Divine syllable
Vayu: air / wind
Dhatu: nature of, aspect of
Hanumanta: Son on Hanuman, the monkey god
Ya: grammatical association

The mind is like a monkey, always jumping everywhere. We aim at mastering our mind so that our thoughts become focused. The monkey god Hanuman is not a person, but a representation of the mastered mind, or the mind taken under our own control, and dominated by our Spirit. Hanumanta is the son of Hanuman, or the result of having a mastered mind. It is the symbol of concentrated thought, and freedom of the mind from false beliefs. If you do not wish to pray to the Hindu god Hanumanta, you may replace it with the angel/spirit of pure mind, named Cittaamala Sattva: Om Vayudhatu Cittaamalasattva

The air mudra: Touch the tip of the pinky finger with the tip of the thumb.

Enhanced charge: Every day, do three malas at the time of sunrise or right after it, then three more at sundown, and three at midnight.

Charging the five elements can take as little as 60 days, if you do 9 malas per day for 12 days, for the five elements in a row. Charging the five elements will awaken every aspect of your spirituality. It will give a biological wisdom to your body. It will open spiritual doors, release blockages, purify your energies.

The five elements are an important part of teaching your mind, heart and body, to interact with nature and go beyond its illusionary limitations. Nature was created with the spiritual concepts of the five elements. It is still operated by the elemental forces.

Charging the five elements will give you the basic tools required to advance much faster in any other training you do; physical, mental or spiritual. It is also encouraged before entering the Siddhi path. Once you have charged the five elements, it is recommended to do activation or support malas, to keep their energies active and intense in your body. Every now and then, do five malas in a row, one mala of each of the five elements.

The five elements must be fully charged before you can start using them. Until you learn how to use these energies, keep them for yourself. They will support every other spiritual action you take. Once you have learned the benefits of the elemental energies, you can use them to treat other people who lack these energies, by touch or transmigration. After a treatment, you must purify your own energies. The amount of time spent in treatment must be balanced by spending the same amount of time chanting the same elemental mantra while putting your hands to the earth. This will purify your energies again.

Always keep the "Heaven" energy for yourself. It is personal and will not bring any benefit to another person.

The Chakra System

Each chakra is a major energy center of the body. Each chakra concerns an aspect of our life. They are not tubes and channels like we would like to imagine them. They are organs, and they are not hollow. This book does not aim at presenting the chakra system. You should review the chakra system by means of your own research. The web is filled with information on the chakra system. Here, we resume the chakras for you, so you know where to put your attention when we will instruct you at a later time.

Each Chakra has a primary function. You will get to know them as you gain experience using the chakra system. These will be described along with the techniques that activate those functions. There are seven major Chakras.

1- Base Chakra: Located at the base of the spine; extends from the base of the pelvis at the front of your body, to the coccyx at the back of your body. The base Chakra thus covers the entire base of your body, centered at the perineum, between your anus and sexual organs.

2- Navel Chakra: Located about one inch below your navel.

3- Solar Plexus Chakra: Located at the solar plexus, right under your sternum.

4- Heart Chakra: Located directly in the middle of the sternum, in front of your heart.

5- Throat Chakra: Located in the little indentation of bones at the front base of your throat.

6- Third Eye Chakra: Located between your eyebrows.

7- Crown Chakra: Found at the top of your head, with the center point exactly on top of your head, but spreading down to surround part of your head, around the forehead and the back of the skull.

Another important Chakra is called the "Jade Gate", and it is found at the back of the head, on the pointy bone at the back of the skull. It is not an extension of the third eye, crossing the body like the other chakras do.

Behind the Navel Chakra, in the middle of the body, inside the lower abdomen, is a place called the "Dan-tian" in Chinese Medicine; we will refer to it in our practices. It is in the Dan-tian where the energy of the body is gathered and stored for later use.

It is not necessary to remember all these Chakras right now. We will give you the information you need about the Chakras throughout the book.

3 Suns

The three suns are one sun, perceived at three different places in the body, in three different ways, contemplating three philosophical concepts, but still, it is only one sun. The technique is simple enough. Sit and prepare for meditation.

First sun: Start by visualizing a glorious sun in your third eye. If you have trouble with this, you can start with a distant sun that comes closer and closer to you, and ends in between your brows. Keep the view of a glorious sun in your third eye. Pull your physical eyes up a bit, without effort, to focus on your third eye. Recite the mantra "OOOOOMMMMMM" in your mind.

The highest level of Divine energy in the universe resonates with the mantra OM. Do this technique by itself at least once for 20 minutes, before moving on to the second sun.

Second sun: Once you did at least one simple 20 minute meditation with the first sun, you can work on activating the second sun. Start with the visualization of the first glorious sun in your third eye, and recite the mantra OM once. Keep your physical eyes gently pointing towards your third eye. Then, visualize a radiant sun in your solar plexus. The goal is to keep both the glorious sun in your third eye, and the energy radiant sun in your solar plexus. Use the image you wish to make a difference between the glorious and radiant sun. If you have trouble keeping both suns in your mind, alternate between them. Now, you will use the mantra "Om Vajra".

The highest energy of the spiritual realm is called Vajra. It is indestructible, ever shining light. When compared to a stone, it is diamond. When compared to a metal, it is adamantium. When compared to a natural phenomenon, it is a thunderbolt. The V of Vajra is a percuted V, that sounds almost like a B. Saying this mantra as "Bajra" would be too hard, but in some Hindu communities, it is spoken Bajra, even if written Vajra.

The mantra OM is associated to the first, glorious and divine sun, in the third eye. The mantra Vajra is associated to the second energy radiant sun, in the solar plexus. Keep both images of the sun at once, or alternate between them until you can keep both in mind. Do at least one 20 minute meditation with the two first suns.

Third sun: Invoke the first sun in your third eye. Mentally recite the mantra OM. Pause at this step for a few seconds. Then, invoke the second sun in your solar plexus. Mentally recite the mantra Om Vajra. Pause again. Now, at your base chakra, visualize a thermal magma sun. Keeping the image of the three suns in your mind, splitting your attention at the three concerned chakras (third eye, solar plexus, base chakra), mentally recite the mantra "Om Vajra Agni".

The highest energy force in nature is fire. Fire is said "Agni" in Sanskrit. Each of the four letters of A-G-N-I should be distinctly pronounced when you recite the mantra Agni. In some languages, the "gn" is a single upper palatale sound. It is not so in Sanskrit, so the "G" and the the "N" should be distinguished, even if only a little, when you recite the mantra.

Keep the image of the three suns in your mind, all at once. When you get used to it, try to imagine that it is the same unique sun, represented in three places, each with their quality: the divine glorious sun, the spiritual energy radiant sun, and the natural thermal magma sun.

When you are ready, you can charge the "Om Vajra Agni" mantra in the fashion of 9 malas per day for 12 days, or 3 malas a day for 36 days.

Vajrayana

The Buddha was not a Buddhist, but a Hindu. He attained enlightenment thru the studies of the Vedas, the practice of meditation and yoga. Amongst esoteric Buddhist practices, there is a lot of the Hindu heritage to Buddhism. What is now called Vajrayana, or the Vehicule of Vajra, is what was once a set of rituals for the Hindu god Indra, holder of the power of Vajra. The Buddhists, wanting to contemplate the inner self more than the outer gods, stripped out any reference to Indra, and included references to many Buddhas who showed the way of Vajra. The esoteric wisdom of Vajrayana traveled out of India, like every other Buddhist tradition, into China, Tibet, Japan, and all other surrounding countries. The most knowledgeable people on Vajrayana today are the Tibetans. However, a specific technique of Vajrayana, composed of nine mudras and mantras, found more adepts in China and Japan. This technique became known as "Kuji-In" in Japan, and was practiced by warriors as well as priests, for its efficient way to awaken the Vajra power within the practitioner.

Here we will quickly review the Kuji-In process. Those who feel attracted to Kuji-In should find more information on the website www.Kujiin.com.

Kuji-In Technique Overview

Kuji-In is translated from the Japanese as "Nine Syllables". The number nine is the number that symbolizes completion in the Buddhist system. Your hands are your primary tool in these practices, and each hand mudra is combined with a specific mantra/sound, mandala/visualization and breathing exercise that completes the technique. Thus, each set is comprised of a mudra/mantra/mandala, and will be referred to as a SET for the remainder of this text. The Kuji-In technique is composed of nine SETS.

In Kuji-In practice you will be combining these three components (mudra, mantra and mandala) in order to manifest your desires. Remember that your goal for now is to perform the daily practices for the joy of learning these techniques and for the pleasure of connecting to your Divine Self. For each SET you will make the hand signs (mudra), say the single word repeatedly (mantra), and visualize the effect of the set to the best of your knowledge (mandala). Start with the first set, (the RIN Mantra), using only that one syllable mantra. Repeat this mantra in your mind, while you also position your hands according to the mudra, and focus your mind on the concept associated with the mudra/mantra. Focus without conscious effort. Let your mind simply settle down until it rests on that thought. Do not judge yourself harshly if your mind wanders in every direction; simply come back peacefully to the practice.

Do not move on to the next set until you are comfortable with the three parts of the first set: get comfortable with using your hands (mudra), together with the indicated word (mantra) and thought (mandala). When you master the three parts of a single set, and you feel that something is starting to happen in the energy planes, you can move to the next set. Each set may take as little as a day, or as much as a month of daily practice before you can feel its effect. Practice periods may vary between five minutes and an hour every day. If you don't feel anything after a few days of practice, move on to the next set. Eventually, you will feel the energies actively working on your body.

When you reach the ninth set, you will start learning more complex mantras; these are complete prayers. At this juncture it is best that you begin with the first set again and re-climb the ladder. This will greatly enhance the efficiency of your Kuji-In practices, and the Divine Forces will be more present to work with you during your practices. This form of mantra is a prayer, thus it is uttered repeatedly with faith. Say it just as you would speak any normal phrase that deserves to be spoken with reverence. It is to your True Self that you are praying.

Before you begin each practice period, start with a few minutes of the general breathing exercise. Then, for each practice period, start with the first set (RIN), and continue with each set in sequence for one full minute, followed by the next set (for one minute) , one after the other, until you reach the set that you are currently learning/working on. You may practice the set you are currently working on for as long as you wish.

Once you have gone through the process of learning the entire Kuji-In system, a normal practice period can be accomplished over thirty minutes as follows: One minute of breathing, three minutes per set (total twenty-seven minutes), and two minutes of silent contemplation. You may then meditate for another half hour to elevate your consciousness.

In the following presentation, the first photo demonstrates the best way to do each exercise and the second photo shows you the proper finger placement for that exercise. The instructions for each mudra are followed by the Chakra associated with that set, the mantra prayer to be spoken with it, and the concepts and benefits associated with practicing the set.

Here is a list of the 9 Kuji-In sets with their japanese titles, associating each with their popular benefits.

1- RIN – Reinforces the positive aspects of the physical, mental and energetic planes.
2- KYO – Increases the healthy flow of energy, mastery of energy.
3- TOH – Enhances your positive relationship with the universe, resulting in improved harmony and balance.

4- SHA – Develops enhanced healing, regeneration.

5- KAI– Develops foreknowledge, premonition, intuition, feeling.

6- JIN – Increases telepathic ability, communication, knowledgeability.

7- RETSU – Enhances your perception and mastery of space-time dimensions.

8- ZAI – Fosters a relationship with the Elements of creation.

9- ZEN – Results in Enlightenment, completeness, suggestive invisibility.

Although the only apparent features would be the commonly seated posture holding some kind of hand position, this Nine Hand Seals method actually combines five main tools:

- a hand position, called "mudra" in sanskrit
- a spoken expression, called "mantra" in sanskrit
- a focus point in the body, called "chakra" in sanskrit
- a mental visualization, called "mandala" in sanskrit
- a philosophical concept to ponder

1- RIN

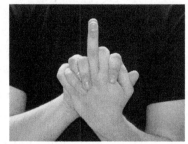

Extend your two middle fingers and interlace all other fingers.

Chakra: Base

Mantra: Om vajramanataya swaha

The RIN set is used to strengthen your mind and body. This Kuji-in set must be performed before any other Kuji-in sets can truly be effective. The RIN Kuji acts as a sort of hook-up to the Ultimate Source of all Power. By connecting you with this Divine energy, the RIN Kuji strengthens your mind and body, especially in collaboration with the other practices of the Kuji-In. A stronger connection to the Divine energy source will make you stronger at every level. Please be aware that this set may elevate your body temperature.

2- KYO

 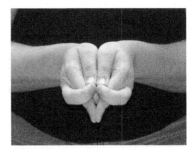

Extend your index fingers and bend your middle fingers over your index fingers so that the tip of your thumbs are touching. Interlace all your other fingers.

Chakra: Hara/Navel
Mantra: Om ishaanayaa yantrayaa swaha

KYO activates the flow of energy within your body and outside of you, in your environment. This Kuji will help you learn to direct energy throughout your body, and eventually outside your body, so you can manifest your desires in the objective world. Although willpower directs energy, you must not push too hard with your willpower. Willpower that is used to direct energy should be rather like "wanting something a lot" but not like "getting a stranglehold on something, or pushing with a crippling force". Even when you apply your willpower to attain something you desire, you must always be at peace and relaxed.

3- TOH

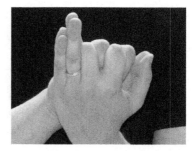

Point your thumbs and the last two fingers of both hands while keeping your index and middle fingers interlaced inside your hands.

Chakra: Dan-tian, between the Hara and the Solar Plexus
Mantra: Om jitraashi yatra jivaratna swaha

By practicing TOH, you will develop your relationship with your immediate environment, and eventually with the entire universe. As you practice, begin by filling yourself with energy and then surround yourself with this energy. (This is accomplished by visualizing that it is so). This is the Kuji of harmony. It teaches you to accept the outside events of life while remaining at peace inside. Always breathe deeply inside your abdomen, naturally, without strain.

4- SHA

Extend your thumbs, index fingers and both little fingers. Interlace your middle and fourth finger inside your hands.

Chakra: Solar Plexus
Mantra: Om haya vajramaantayaa swaha

With this Kuji, the healing ability of your body is increased. As you practice this set, your body will become more efficient in its daily rebuilding, healing and reconstruction. This increased healing efficiency is the result of the higher levels of energy passing through your energy channels (Meridians) and your solar plexus. This healing vibration will eventually radiate around you, causing other people to heal as you spend time with them.

5- KAI

 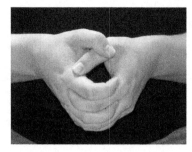

Interlace all of your fingers, with the tip of each finger pressing into the root of the facing finger.

Chakra: Heart
Mantra: Om namah samanta vajranam ham

This Kuji will raise your awareness and help you to develop your intuition. The mudra is called "The outer bonds". The outer bonds are the energy currents that precede every event, if only for an instant. They are the specific influence from the outside world that produces every one of your experiences.

Intuition is a powerful ally; it is the way you perceive what your senses register from your contact with the environment, and from the people surrounding you. This set will increase your intuition and will help you to learn to love yourself and others.

6- JIN

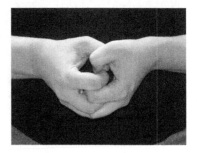

Interlace all your fingers, with your fingertips inside, each of them touching the equivalent tip of the other hand's finger, if possible.

Chakra: Throat

Mantra: Om agnayaa yanmayaa swaha

The "inner bonds" are the energy currents inside you that connect you with your True Self. We have the ability to know what others are thinking. By reaching deep inside you, into the place with no words, you may get in contact with this same place in others. When you make this connection you may hear the other person's thoughts without words, or you may learn to communicate by thought concepts; this is commonly called telepathy.

This mudra is used to open your mind to the thoughts that others project from their mental activity. It can help you gain an understanding of why people do the things they do. If you don't judge what you perceive, you will perceive it with more clarity.

7- RETSU

Point your left index finger up. Wrap the fingers of your right hand around your left index finger. Place the tips of your right thumb and index finger in contact with the tip of your left index finger. The fingers of your left hand are gathered into a fist.

Chakra: Jade Gate, at the back of the head
Mantra: Om jyota-hi chandoga jiva tay swaha

After practicing the Kuji-In exercises for some time, they will alter your perception of gross matter so you will be able to perceive the different flows of energy composing our space-time multi-dimensional universe. Per the theory of relativity, as mass accelerates, time slows, thus if your energy is flowing, and you apply your willpower, your mass accelerates, time slows for you and you can simply change (or direct) the flow/ or motion of your body through space.

Now, put all this theory aside for a moment and let your mind adapt to this new perception of the Universe. Imagine that the atoms of the universe are composed of energy waves instead of rigid, inflexible solid matter.

8- ZAI

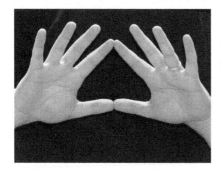

Touch the tips of your thumbs and index fingers to form a triangle, while your other fingers are spread out.

Chakra: Third Eye
Mantra: Om srija iva rtaya swaha

sRija : sh-ree-j with an almost mute "ee" after the R
Rtaya: Rutaya with an almost mute "u" after the R

By practicing with this set, you will establish a relationship with the Universal components of creation: the elements. These elements are not only physical, they are also spiritual. This Kuji practice is a basis for the power of manifestation. Visualize being in harmony with nature. Visualize the flow of Qi from nature to you, and from you to nature. After a while, notice your increasing awareness that nature is alive, and that you can communicate with it. Nature will interact with you within the limits of natural law. Eventually, as you improve your sensitivity to nature, you might develop the ability to call forth an elemental manifestation, when mastered.

9- ZEN

Rest your left knuckles on the fingers of your right hand, with your right palm open. Touch the tips of your two thumbs gently.

Chakra: Crown
Mantra: Om ah ra pa cha na dhi

Illumination is the highest state of mind. Illumination is a kind of Completeness, accomplished by Meditation. By using this practice, you can eventually disappear from the common mind. You are still there, of course, but others in the common mind cannot register your presence, because your vibration is higher than what their minds can recognize or interpret as real. To practice, imagine simple emptiness, calm white light everywhere; Then visualize melding with the white light. It is believed that, to the average person, you might become invisible. Many hours of practice are required to elevate your vibration level enough to manifest the side-effects, like suggestive invisibility.

Relationship with the Divine

Now that you have experienced the spiritual world, you cannot deny that there is something spiritual. There is oneness in the universal soul. There is a supreme THING that encompasses everything, that is the absolute Divine. This, we will call God. Yet the name of "God" is sometimes uncomfortable for some, because it is attached to dogmas, to definitions, and to past experiences, pleasant or not.

Un-define God

In every ancient religion or dogma of the world, spiritual seekers have observed nature and the universe. They have all discovered that there is an absolute truth, which is also intelligent, but has to name, shape, sound, figure or anything else to refer to as a human.

To transmit this vision of the absolute to the common population, the mystics have given a name, shape, sound, figure, and even invented rules to help the population accept the spiritual concept in their minds, without having to do any spiritual work.

The word "God" has been used by every religion and dogma to relate to the un-definable concept of the pre-created, so that people can exchange ideas about this un-definable concept of absolute truth. It is necessary for our human minds to have a word to classify the knowledge about this concept of the universe. The problem occurs when we start to believe that the highest definition about God is the definition accessible with the human mind.

The mind is a level of the human existence, and is not the highest, nor the lowest. The mind is above the emotional level, but below the spiritual level. The highest level of definition of God is accessible to our Spirit, which is higher than the human mind, therefore there is information about God that cannot be grasped by the mind.

To understand the concept of the absolute truth, it is necessary to do a spiritual movement within, to contemplate this spiritual truth even if it seems un-accessible to the human mind at first. As long as you can forget any pre-conception about God learned thru religion or dogma, you can contemplate the absolute truth without name or shape.

Religion and dogmas have been a necessity for many people, to concentrate their attention on a single point, and hope for spiritual awakening, that would become available to only the elite (hum!?) of such religions. They have used the word "God" to define the absolute truth, and then give it a shape, and sound, a concept, even a right to judge and punish.

It is important to un-define the word "God" so that this word can become available again to represent the absolute truth without name or shape. Forget everything you think you know about God, everything you hold on to reassure yourself that you will go to some "paradise" after your "death".

We will work to help you define a more refined definition of: heaven, hell, earth, life, death, God... This knowledge is occult and will probably destroy everything you believed in so far. You will be free to know and chose your beliefs, and not obliged by some organization or church. We will not tell you our vision of what all of this means, but rather offer you tools for your mind to accept and contribute to your own discovery of the universe and its laws.

Please note that it can be healthy for your spiritual and mental health to participate in religious activities. We simply do not wish you to think it is essential, and that our own dogmas would be better than yours. When you practice your religious activities, do so with a free mind, and do not pay attention to the sectary attitude of other believers.

Prayer

Prayer is essential. Define for yourself what could be the highest concept of the universe, and pray it. Give it the name of your choice. Use the image and concepts of your choice, and pray. In no case should you try to impose your view of the truth to others. Everyone has a distinct view of the universe, of God, of Spirit, or of Truth.

One of the most important aspects of attaining power, is the development of a LOVE relationship with what is the highest thing in the universe, that you cannot define. Being in LOVE with the Divine requires, and develops, faith. Faith is more than self trust. It is certainly not a blind trust in an unseen savior. Faith is not about being saved or relieving your human responsibilities to the Divine. Faith is a feeling of absolute trust in the Spirit. Whatever you do, do it with God. If you don't do it with God, don't do it.

However, faith comes gradually. Do not think you have failed if you are not motivated by absolute faith right from the start. True faith comes with years of practice and gratitude towards the universe. When you pray, do not ask for anything. Rather, be thankful for what you already have, and pray for blessings, without any precision to what the blessings would be.

The Path of Supernatural Powers

The Path of Powers is known in the Hindu tradition as the Siddha path, where they learn about Siddhi, which are the various abilities and powers. Everywhere in books and on the web, you can find series of mantras and techniques, but few or none deliver the desired results. The main reason is that it takes a certain level of training before entering into the Siddha path. Knowing the mantras is not enough.

Supernatural means beyond the natural. What exists beyond nature is what created it. It is the spiritual world of consciousness. If you did not complete the extraneous training so far, you will attain success very slowly with the following training, unless you already have years of a spiritual path behind you. However, since you did do all the trainings suggested yet in this book, you will have some success with the following training within a few months. Thus, it takes patience anyway.

For the following concepts to have any kind of effect, it is essential to have followed most of the training so far. Reading the recipes and knowing all about the ingredients won't turn you into a good chef. You need to practice. More so because the knowledge required for achieving supernatural abilities is not found in this book, but in the realm of consciousness. All the information found in this book is meant to lead you on the path of consciousness so that you can really learn about the mechanism of the universe when you exist consciously as the Self, aware of the realm of consciousness that pervades everything.

Most importantly, it is essential to have:
- Charged the mantra of Peace
- Charged the mantra of Compassion
- Charged the mantra of the Three Suns
- Have experience with Consciousness Transmigration
- Have experience with Emotional Transmutation
- Have experience with the Pure Land mantra
- Understand the importance of the Divine Mother
- Understand the importance of prayer
- Practice a form of empowerment of your choice: Kuji-In, 5 elements, or other.

Charging the elemental mantras is not absolutely essential before you continue, but it will be helpful in attaining the full efficiency of the second Siddhi.

The Siddhis are not charged thru japa, but thru the practice of meditation. Each Siddhi is a single word, accompanied with a philosophical concept to keep in mind throughout the meditation. You need to be sitting still, relaxed. If possible, do not rest your spine on anything. Try to keep your back standing on its own, without putting tension on it. Your spine can be slightly bent for comfort.

Before you have a Siddhi meditation, you have to prepare your Self, soul, mind, heart, and body. Each practice should go as follows:

- Prayer to the unique God, within the tradition of your choice, or in an un-defined manner.
- Recite a mala of your choice (i.e.: the mantra of Peace to calm your mind, three suns for energy…)
- Two minutes of pranayama.
- A minimum of 20 minutes of Siddhi meditation.

Also, when you are done, do not forget to keep a positive attitude, even to recite positive affirmations for at least 20 minutes.

To do a Siddhi meditation, mentally repeat the Siddhi word every few seconds, with a calm neutral attitude. While you keep in mind a calmly paced mantra, contemplate the philosophical concept of the Siddhi. Let the short mantra and the philosophy resonate in your consciousness. Delve inside yourself. Immerse yourself in the world of consciousness.

After a few minutes, let go of the philosophical contemplation, to remain in a state of awareness while you repeat the mantra. Come back to the mental contemplation only if your mind wavers, and then let go again.

I understand the temptation to go as fast as possible thru each of the Siddhis, until you reach the Siddhi that you wish to develop. This would only result in failure. You have to practice each Siddhi, step by step, for a long period of time. You have to meditate with the first Siddhi until you feel its effect in your body and your mind, when you experience something greater than the human self. There is no rule set for this, especially because it is difficult to identify when we are ready to hop onto the next step. You should have a minimum of 20 meditation periods with a single Siddhi before you go to the other. Even if you feel strong spiritual influences, it does not mean that you are done with this Siddhi. You should also have a minimum of one month of practice with each Siddhi. If you are the type of person who rarely feels anything, follow the above rules to orient yourself.

Often, I personally like to come back to the first Siddhi, and do all Siddhis in the form of one per meditation over a period of a month. When I was introduced to the Siddhi meditation process, I used the first Siddhi for 8 years in a row, simply because I was never instructed in any of the other Siddhis. At first, I even thought that the Siddhi meditation consisted of this single mantra. This is what helped me go very far, very quickly, in every other technique I have ever tried since then.

There are a few different traditions of the Siddha path, each with their own mantra order. I will instruct you with the path that I have learned. Please do not compare with other paths. They are all good. Yet, stick to a single Siddhi path.

It is important to practice the first 9 Siddhis in a row. I call it the Continuous Path. Then, you can hop to any other Siddhi you wish for in the remaining Siddhis, so to develop a specific supernatural ability. I call these Siddhis the Multiple Paths. Thus, within the first year or so, you should be practicing the continuous path, then, take the Siddhi path of your choice, until you attain success. Once you are done with the continuous path, you will select a single Siddhi to develop one of the multiple paths. You will keep doing this Siddhi practice until you attain visible traces of the coming success. Then, it will be up to you to change to another Siddhi, or to continue for months, or even years, so you can totally manifest your desired supernatural ability.

You are invited to read the complete list of Siddhis, so that you may encourage yourself in persevering in your practice. The Siddhis can manifest quite impressing phenomena, when they are mastered with years of meditation. All along, resist the temptation to go too fast. Travel the path like it was exposed. Or else, it might result in a failure to develop any supernatural ability at all.

Discretion is advised. Although anyone may read about the Siddhis just about everywhere, keeping the mantras silent is a cornerstone of the practice. Each time you will mention the Siddhi aloud, you will impoverish your chances of success with the Siddhi. Instead, when we wish to speak of a specific Siddhi, we call it by its number, or concept. We'd say "The first Siddhi" or "The smallest Siddhi", instead of naming the mantra itself. The energy you put to reserve the use of the mantras to your mental recitation, will be greatly amplifying the effect and speed at which you will develop the Siddhis.

More so, you should not tell anyone at which Siddhi you are at in the continuous path, or which one is your Siddhi of predilection in the multiple path. This entire process must remain personal.

In the tradition where I was shown the Siddhi path, it was strictly forbidden to even say the mantras with the mouth, unless it was by a teacher at the moment of teaching it. Otherwise, no one ever told any mantra aloud. You should develop this level of reverence for your own development.

WARNING: The Siddhis are meant to expand your consciousness and help you evolve as a spiritual being. They all deliver side-effects very interesting to the human animal nature (the ego). If you end up using the Siddhis in ways to harm others, or to acquire goods that are not meant to be yours, the karmic price to pay will be heavier than with other types of offense done thru natural means. These Siddhis are traps for the human ego, to entrain you in acting with virtue. If you see yourself becoming arrogant, pretentious, or driven to do parlor tricks, take a step back and observe yourself. You must remain in control of your human behavior. You must behave with virtue, humility, and with great discernment. Your choices must be driven by a sense of justice and compassion.

The Siddhis

The Continuous path

1. ANIMA

The first Siddhi is "Anima". It is a Sanskrit word that means "Smallest". It is not the same word as the latin "anima" that means Self or Soul. The Sanskrit ANIMA refers to the smallest, most refined substance into which all things dwell. Every atom, every particle or wave, bathes in this infinitely smaller substance. This substance is your God. When you pray to the Christ, this is the universal Christ pervading everything. In the Hindu path, we think that "Vishnu pervades the universe entirely". Everything is made from, and within Vishnu. Everything is made from, and bathes in the Highest Self, the highest consciousness. During the meditation on the first Siddhi, recite the word over and over, thinking of the smallest substance that is everywhere. Your mind might waver between a small point to think of the smallest, and then on the size of the universe to imagine it pervades everything. You can use such concepts to help you start, but quickly, you should forget about a single point, or the whole of the universe. Simply contemplate that the Highest Consciousness that is God, is all pervading.

2. MAHIMA

The second Siddhi is "Mahima" which means "greatest, biggest". While you recite the mantra-word, thinking of the biggest thing or force, contemplate the five elements. You can browse thru the five elements one at a time, or all together continually. Remember that the five elements are not the coarse physical manifestation, but the five conceptual energies that created everything. If you repeat words in your mind like "earth, fire, heaven, water, air" you will be inhibiting the effect of the mantra-word itself. Thus, you can start the meditation by remembering the concepts of the five elements using words, but quickly go to the un-worded concept of the five elements, and repeat only the Siddhi word MAHIMA. During this practice, you will contemplate that the five elements are Vishnu, the Christ, the created universe. The son of God, that was the all-substance during the practice of "Anima", now is the spiritual energy of the five elements, in the form of the biggest energies of the universe.

3. GARIMA

The third Siddhi is "Garima", which means "heavy". It not only refers to weight, but also to gravity and all other types of natural forces. During the practice of this Siddhi, do not only contemplate the concept of heaviness, but also on the concept of the pulling force, the attracting magnetism, and the atomic forces. Vishnu/Christ/Buddha is the force of the universe in operation.

4. LAGHIMA

"Laghima" means "light weight", or weightlessness. It is a state of mind where the previous forces that operates the universe are set free, liberated from any attachment, from any bond. During this Siddhi, contemplate that the Vishnu/Christ/Buddha is the force that freely drives the five elements in the universe. The son of God is the energy and power behind the five elements. Feel light, feel the lightness, feel the driving force behind the universal elements.

5. PRAPTI

"Prapti" means "Reach" in some circumstances, and "Obtain" in others. It is about our capacity to reach our goals. This Siddhi gives us the ability to obtain anything we set out minds to. During this Siddhi meditation, contemplate that the Vishnu/Christ/Buddha is the source of our ego. All that we are, in human nature, is created by the source of all things.

6. PRAKAMYA

"Prakamya" means "Irresistible will". This Siddhi give the ultimate willpower. It provides the drive to accomplishing anything, with determination and unaltered perseverance. Meditate on Vishnu/Christ/Buddha as the Sepreme Self that is the single consciousness that flows thru all beings.

7. ISHITVA

"Ishitva" means "supremacy". In nature, animals tend to feel the radiance of authority of other animals. It is not only determinant in the food chain, but even amongst a pack, it influences hierarchy. Those with lesser radiance will naturally respect those with more radiance. This Siddhi provides such a radiance of supremacy, of kingship, and it will provide an influence in your relationships with others. This is one of the ego traps. At high levels, it is also thru this Siddhi that one acquires the ability to control the illusion and the senses of others. During this Siddhi meditation, contemplate that the Supreme Self, the Vishnu/Christ/Buddha, is the controller of the illusion of the senses in all beings. You must focus on the Supreme Self, beyond your human nature.

8. VASHITVA

"Vashitva" means something close to "One's own will", and implied freedom of will, and the domination of others' will. This Siddhi is accomplished by meditating on the Supreme Self being the commander of the universe. It is, however, the biggest trap of the Siddha path. When used to prevent others' free-will, the karmic impact is immediate and tenfold. You should use this Siddhi to free yourself and others.

9. KAAMARUTATTVA

"Kaamarutattva" means "Consummation of all true desires". With this Siddhi, all the desires that you really hold true, will be accomplished, or manifest by themselves. Only authentic desires will manifest. If you think you would like to have lots of money, but deep inside, your real desire is to have security in the form of a stable roof, then a house might manifest itself, without the money, or just with enough money for the house. Try to identify your real desires. This Siddhi is accomplished by meditating on the Creator as an omnipresent force, expanding and transcending reality. The

Creator is Bramha, or the Father, or Amitabha Buddha, and it is everpresent, everywhere, transcending reality.

Here ends the continuous path. If you go thru this path within less than nine months, do not expect miracles. If you spend one year per Siddhi, meditating everyday, you will certainly accomplish them. Or, you could go thru them on a monthly basis, and come back to them afterwards. Practicing the Siddhi meditation develops faith, since you are continually contemplating your higher self, and the Supreme Self.

From time to time, I like to review all the basic Siddhis. I sit to meditate, prepare myself accordingly, then I start with the first Siddhi, and spend around 5 minutes on each. Since I don't really time myself, I end up meditating for 45 to 60 minutes. Yet, most of the time, I will come to a point where I will simply transcend. Transcending is a goal to attain. The more your transcend, the more you will eventually transcend consciously, becoming the Higher Self and retain consciousness of it.

The Multiple Paths

I will list the Siddhis of the multiple paths with less detail. Once you are done with the continuous path, all the following will make sense, and before that, no explanation will make any. Just do it. The Siddhis will be explained in the form of Siddhi: explanation; technique.

All references to the Supreme Being, the Supreme Self, Vishnu/Christ/Buddha, are all the same. Then, there are references to the Self and Highest Self, which is more likely to be your individual spiritual nature at the highest level, even though this too, is one with the Supreme Self.

A lot of practice is required for these Siddhis to manifest. A few recitations of a mantra will not compensate the ages spend away from the true nature of the Self. However, to the diligent and perseverant meditator, results come fast enough. Do not attempts any feats that could be damageable for yourself or others, before you completely master a Siddhi.

Anumi Mattvam: absence of thirst, hunger, disease, misery, old age and death; meditate on the Supreme Self in your human self, being the embodiment of virtue. You must also be neutral in your life, to be unaffected by nature.

Sravana Darsanam: to see and hear from distance; meditates on the Supreme Self as the transcendent sound which pulses through air and space, the sun that lights up the universe, the eye that sees and the light of both the sun and the eye. It is all vibration, and all its interaction with the senses. It is light, sound, and perception united in a single consciousness.

Manah Javah: means "swift mind", used to to move the body as fast as the mind wills it; meditates on the Supreme Self as the unifier of body, breath and mind.

Vayu Gaman: Through this Siddhi a person can become capable of flying in the skies and traveling from one place to another in just a few seconds; First, accomplish levitation using the Laghima and Manah Javah Siddhis a lot, then use the same meditation concepts for this Siddhi. Once it is acquired, use this Siddhi along with the transmigration technique to teleport yourself.

Kama Rupam: to assume a desired form; meditate on the Supreme Self as the one form that becomes the many.

Parakaya Pravesanam: to transmigrate into another's body; meditate on yourself being the force that transmigrates into another body through Prana.

Svachanda Mrtyu: to die according to one's own will; comes to the Yogi who learned the art of occluding the anus with his heel, channeling the prana from the heart to the place in the crown known as Brahma randhara (middle of forehead, between the third eye and the crown chakra) and returning to any Chakra as he desires, with his own will.

Sahakridanu-darsanam: to play with gods; meditate on the true nature of the Self, the Highest Self.

Yatha Sankalpa Samsiddhi: to accomplish one's will and wish; will come to those who have full faith in the Supreme Self, knowing that the will of God is always accomplished.

Ajnaprathihata Gati: to have others obey one's will; merge with the self-contained oneness of the Supreme Being, Vishnu/Christ/Buddha, in which all things move.

Tri Kala Jnatvam: to know the past, present and future; comes to one who has purified himself completely, and mastered the art of meditation in fixity.

Advandvam: to be immune to cold and heat, joy and misery, pain and pleasure; comes to one who has attained complete tranquility thru devotion to God. Neutrality is required.

Para Citta Abhijnata: to read others' thoughts and mind; comes to who is free from the bounds of human conditioning, by relying only on God.

Agnyarkambuvishadinam: to counteract the injury caused by fire, sun, water, poison; comes to one who has absolute faith in God, and exists in a completely neutral, detached attitude.

Pratsihtambho aparajaya: not to succumb to any one; comes to one who has absolute faith in God, and exists in a completely neutral, detached attitude.

Haadi: On acquiring this Vidya (wisdom) a person neither feels hungry nor thirsty and he can remain without eating food or drinking water for several days at a stretch; meditate on the Supreme Being sustaining all the needs.

Kaadi: Just as one does not feel hungry or thirsty in Haadi Vidya similarly in Kaadi Vidya a person is not affected by change of seasons i.e. by summer, winter, rain etc. After accomplishing this Vidya a person shall not feel cold even if he sits in the snow laden mountains and shall not feel hot even if he sits in the fire; meditate on the Supreme Being sustaining the body in all its functions.

Kanakdhara: one can acquire immense and unlimited wealth through this Siddhi; meditate on the Divine Mother caring for all your needs, providing beyond your needs, and the experience of gratitude.

Pararupagati: Motion of a distant form; Practice a lot of Laghima, Manah Javah, and transmigration. Then, develop this Siddhi by meditating on the Supreme Self being the operator of all motion in the universe.

There are many other Siddhis, such as manifestation or resurrection of the dead, that require more than meditation on a concept while repeating a mantra. We will cover more supernatural abilities in the next chapter.

Sri Swami Sivananda offers a word of advice, from his paper Satsanga and Svadhyaya: Siddhis are no True Criterion of True Spirituality

« Another great blunder people generally commit is that they judge the enlightenment of Sadhus by the Siddhis they display. In the world generally, the common inclination is to judge the merits and ability of a Sadhu through his Siddhis. It is a blunder indeed. They should not judge the enlightenment of a Sadhu in this way.

Siddhis are by-products of concentration. Siddhis have nothing to do with Self-realisation. A Sadhu may manifest Siddhis due to strong passions and intense desires, and if that be the case, he is undoubtedly a big householder only. You must believe me when I tell you that Siddhis are a great hindrance to spiritual progress, and so long as one is within the realm of Siddhis and does not try to rise above it and march onwards, there is not the least hope of God-realisation for him. But, this does not mean that a person manifesting Siddhis is not a realised soul. There are several instances of such persons who have exhibited several Siddhis purely for the elevation and uplift of the world, but never for selfish motives.

During the days of Sri Ramakrishna Paramahamsa Dev, a certain Sadhu approached him and showed two Siddhis: one was that he could roam about without being seen by anybody. The other was that light emanated from his anus when he walked. This man after some time entered the apartments of a lady unseen, misused his power, fell in love with her and lost his two powers. In the world generally, the common run of people and even educated persons judge Sadhus by their Siddhis only. It is a serious blunder and hence I seriously warn you. »

I will also inform you of a similar warning, by exposing a personal experience. I had acquired the ability to influence nature, to make it rain or not, to make it wind or not. After experiencing alone, I repeated the feat with some friends. Even if I tried to master my attitude very hard, a thought came to me right before a representation to some friends, that sounded like "Hey, look at me and my power!". Immediately, I lost all ability to have any form of influence over nature. I felt very stupid, and this event created a whole set of reactions on the part of these friends.

As long as you feel the need to receive attention from other people, you will hinder your progress on the path of supernatural abilities. Take some time, every day, to pay attention to yourself. Give yourself the attention you wish for. Rejoice when you spend time with others, but come to depend only on yourself. It is healthy to have a family and friends, but you must still take care of yourself. Love yourself as much as you can. If you find it hard to do, then practice emotional transmutation as much as you can.

Supreme Powers

The following Sri Siddhis require complete training systems on their own. And for some part of them, the explanation can only be found in the repeated experience of the Higher Self; hence the importance of meditation. Here, we will view the resumed and reduced wisdom that concern them. In time, and as I get a sufficient level of success with each of these Sri Siddhis, I will write complete books on each subject alone. As of now, these are the Supreme Power said only to be available to the most accomplished enlightened beings.

Influencing nature

Nature is inhabited by nature spirits. Every tradition called them many different names, and we will not state them at the moment. Each type of nature spirit responds positively to a virtuous behavior, and is offended by a degraded behavior. For example, the Khacara spirit of the air are appealed by wisdom and discernment, but are offended by arrogance and vanity. The more virtuous you behave, the better nature will react to your calls.

Then, to call the forces of nature, you must not use words from your dictionary, but an attitude in your mind combined with a feeling in your heart. This mindset and feeling is projected outwards as an expression of the self. From there, the nature spirits will receive your message in a language they understand. Knowing the names of the various nature spirits is only useful for you, to help you organize your thoughts. In nature language, if you wish to address yourself to the rain/water spirits, simply tune into this mindset and feeling.

To influence nature, you must be able to expand yourself beyond the limitations of your physical form. Having practiced the two first Siddhis of the continuous path, now practice yourself at expanding your consciousness into the sky. Dissolve your human definition for a moment. Become the sky. From there, get in contact with the nature spirits. Then, focus on the desired result by tuning your thoughts and feelings. If you have developed the virtues required to interact with the appropriate forces of nature, they will influence the natural laws so to replicate your desire as much as possible.

Depending on the power of the influence and the speed of its manifestation, you may spend from 2 minutes to 2 hours in the same mindset/feeling, while consciously expanded in nature. The spirits have to feel you respect nature. They must also feel your faith in God and self-trust.

Telekinesis

The practice of telekinesis requires that you first develop all the techniques found in this book up to the end of the Siddhi Continuous Path. There are also Siddhis that will assist you with telekinesis.

Once you have developed yourself quite enough in the Siddhis, transmigrate your consciousness to become an object, and while being physically anchored to an object, move in the desired direction. It will help to practice the fourth (Laghima) and the unifier (Manah Javah) Siddhis.

I will write a complete telekinesis training book when I have attained sufficient success with this technique. I have attained little results so far (not absence of result, but little).

Power of Manifestation

The power of manifestation ranges from influencing events in your life, to creating tangible matter out of the void. As for influencing events in your life, the Siddhis of the Continuous Path will bring you to that.

Now, let's talk about the creation of tangible matter, manifested from the void of the spiritual realms.

Scientists today have created a simple device that creates new matter, out of nothing. They simply put a powerful pump at the end of a sturdy glass box, and try to empty the air. When the air inside the glass box comes to almost a complete void, new hydrogen atoms pop out of nothingness, like if the all-pervading energy of the universe was pulled from the void into existence.

My experiences with creation of tangible matter out of the spiritual realms, without any other tools than mantras and concentration, have been conclusive enough for me, even though the amount of matter was extremely small. I have created 2 small grains of soil yet, at the moment I am writing this text. It took me 82 days of daily work, and I already have quite some spiritual experience. I have not recorded this information and there are no witnesses. In this sense, at this moment I will write about what I know and what I have experienced, but I will be writing a complete book on the subject when I have become successful enough, with scientifically valid data.

To manifest tangible matter, you have to first empower yourself. It takes so much energy to create matter, that it is impossible for a human being to accumulate this amount of energy into his own system. We have to empower ourselves only to be able to support the activity of the Spirit when it comes to participate in the manifestation. Only the Spirit, one with the universe, can push down the required amount of energy. This is done thru charging and maintaining the five elements. Practicing Kuji-In for a long time will greatly help in the intensity and fluidity of the manifestation process.

Then, you have to acquire the imprint of the consciousness of the matter you wish to manifest. It is the same as acquiring a copy of the data you want to copy on your computer. To manifest matter, you first need to hold in your consciousness the vibration of the matter to duplicate, or manifest. This is done by meditating on the physical composition of the matter to duplicate, without spending too much attention on the actual atomic structure, but trying to feel / sense the consciousness that structures this kind of matter. The Siddhi continuous path helps develop the tools that will permit you to acquire the consciousness imprint of some matter. Strangely enough, organic matter (soil/dirt) is easier to create than simple periodic-structured matter (metals/gems).

After that, you need to establish an extremely good relationship with the Mother Universe, the Divine feminine universal force. Everything was created in the Divine mother, and thru the Divine Mother only can we manifest. The truth is that She is the one manifesting, not our own little ego. This requires that we pray to the Divine Mother every day.

Then, we need to awaken our Bramha / Creator consciousness. It consists in awakening and elevating our consciousness up to the level of the Spirit. This means we must awaken our causal / consciousness body, then gain the awareness of our soul, then of our Spirit, and be united in the Self. This is done thru the practice of the Siddhi process, and Atma Yoga, which is beyond the scope of this book.

Now, with all this done, we can hope to experiment on manifestation. Up to now, this is what we have:

- We have the Brahma / Creator consciousness
- We have a strong relationship with the Divine Mother
- We consciously hold an imprint of the matter we wish to duplicate
- Our human nature is strong enough to support the energies of such a process

At this point, we use mantras of manifestation, with an intense focus on the projecting of the consciousness signature of the matter to reproduce, into the physical realm. The entire process can take quite a while. We have to suck the desired imprint into the physical existence, and project it from the

Spirit. This is not done with mental effort. During the manifestation process, the only effort that the mind does is to keep its focus completely on the object of the experience. It is our Self that makes the effort to come down to the material reality. And our human self must completely let way to our spiritual nature.

You have here all that it takes to entrain yourself at becoming a creator. The specific prayers and practices that I personally use to manifest will be shown to those who have the discipline and courage to go far on their spiritual path.

Material Transmutation

The power of transmutation would require the same expertise than does the power of manifestation, at a lower level. The power of transmutation requires that one taps into the consciousness of a matter to transmute, while focusing on the consciousness imprint of the target matter to obtain. This power is currently used in various methods of environmental purification thru meditation and ritual techniques. It is the same as the alchemist quest to transmute lead into gold. Masters at Emotional Transmutation will have a better idea of the material transmutation process.

Resurrection of the Dead

The resurrection of the Dead is a popular subject of supernatural abilities. It always shows up in the most desired powers of every new student. As of yet, only a few people attained this ability. Their lives and feats are well documented. In the Christian realm, it is believed that there was only one capable of such feats. In the Hindu realm, a lot more people are known to have done such things. Once you have attained great success with the Siddhis of the Continuous Path, and developed great faith in God, then can you start to ponder on the possibilities of brining someone back to life. I will tell here what I know of the science of resurrection.

It is believed that even those who have success in resurrecting dead people may do so only three times during their entire lifetime.

I have not personally experimented on the subject. I have only prevented one of my son's death. He was poisoned at the age of 1 year, eating something toxic: a red appealing flower berry that is known to kill an adult within a few hours. I drove him to the local hospital, where the deadly intoxication was confirmed. He had to be transferred to the big city hospital. Before my son was taken away from my eyesight, I felt his life slowly going away. Then he was put in an ambulance with his mother. When he was in the ambulance, I was driving behind, in my car. Although driving, I started to invoke all the power in the universe, all the forces I had built a relationship with, to keep my son alive. My wife confirmed that at some point during the transport in the ambulance, everything became fine, and all was left to do was for my son to purify his blood. The pain had gone away, and the life was again flowing normally in his body.

The science of resurrection is a bit more intense than the science of keeping someone alive. You must first build relationships with the Divine world. You must tie yourself to as many anchor points in the heavens as you can. This means that you must be knowledgeable in religious and spiritual matters, and have spent a lot of time in meditation, and ritual processes.

When someone dies, the body seems to be dead the moment that the breath and heartbeat stops, but for a while, the body is only in a pre-death lethargy. Within a few hours of the clinical death, the bodily functions can be re-booted.

First, the physical body must still be able to support life. If half of the organs are destroyed, it would require a lot of the body to be re-manifested, which has not been observed, even in the life of the greatest saints. If the body can still support life, like in the case of deaths on impact or drowning, it is thinkable to attempt a resurrection, by very experienced spiritual being.

Then, the soul of the subject must also be willing to continue living in this life, in this body. This is almost always the case. Be available to perceive otherwise, if this is not the case. Your mind will want the soul to come back. But the mind is incapable of perceiving the soul. Only one with an awakened soul can deal with another soul. There is a yoga of the soul (Atma Yoga) that can instruct you in this matter. I teach Atma Yoga to my most advanced students.

The body and soul conditions being met, it is now possible to attempt the resurrection. The first step would be to use the common bonds that the subject had with the physical world. A loved person standing close is advisable, although this person must be able to focus on the love, and not the death. It would also be advisable to have some food that the subject likes a lot. This food will have to be eaten after the resurrection takes place, to re-activate all the bodily functions. It should be healthy and tasty food. But if chocolate is the strongest link, also give chocolate to the re-living. Even after the resurrection, keep the life bonds close until the security of the bodily functions are confirmed.

Then, the life energy of the subject's body must be refilled. A powerful Qi-Gong master can do this, as well as a trained meditator that keeps his own body in very good health. A soft flow of energy, typical of most holistic healers and meditators, will simply not suffice. It takes a spiritual lightning power surge, typical in practitioners of martial arts, Tai-Chi, Vajrayana, or Kuji-In.

Then comes the time of the awakening, where there is a spiritual and physical call to the subject to live. The resurrectionist should take both hands of the subject with his own hands, and pull intensively on the being to come back to life. Focus, concentration, passion, heartfelt love, intense life energy, complete and absolute faith, are all required to bring someone back to life. Resurrection cannot be accomplished by just about anyone. So much parameters are involved that one needs to master himself greatly in order to accomplish such a feat.

I have seen and experimented myself enough supernatural events that I am available to believe in the possibilities of resurrection. It is also of public domain that people got back to life after long periods of clinical death. If I ever experiment with resurrection, if I ever get to this level of expertise, I will give more information on the subject and all my students will be informed.

Conclusion

Training ESP and supernatural abilities takes more than good will. It takes patience, endurance, determination. Just anybody can start to train ESP, but only those who have learned how to dominate the human nature, will have the grace of the Spirit to influence the natural laws. Only by God may nature be truly perceived, influenced, modified, or created. If you think that this training is dangerous in the wrong hands, do not worry. Only by dominating envy, and freeing oneself from greed, can one attain the gifts of obtaining. Only by dominating passions and the senses, can one obtain the gifts of influence. Where the instinct of nature dominates, Spirit is simply not active. Only Spirit is above nature. Without Spirit, there are no supernatural feats. However, it is easy to develop supernatural abilities when engaged on a spiritual path.

I pray that you will find and attain, throughout your training, the greatest value of all things, the most precious jewel, the highest mountain peak, which is the Self.

Be blessed on your path,

MahaVajra

F.Lepine Publishing

Copyright 2008

ISBN: 978-0-9809415-5-5

www.MahaVajra.BE